TWENTIETH CENTURY INTERPRETATIONS
OF

POE'S TALES

TWENTIETH CENTURY INTERPRETATIONS
OF

POE'S TALES

A Collection of Critical Essays

Edited by
WILLIAM L. HOWARTH

Prentice-Hall, Inc. *Englewood Cliffs, N. J.*

A SPECTRUM BOOK

Current printing (last number):

10 9 8 7 6 5 4 3 2 1

PRENTICE-HALL INTERNATIONAL, INC. (*London*)
PRENTICE-HALL OF AUSTRALIA, PTY. LTD. (*Sydney*)
PRENTICE-HALL OF CANADA, LTD. (*Toronto*)
PRENTICE-HALL OF INDIA PRIVATE LIMITED (*New Delhi*)
PRENTICE-HALL OF JAPAN, INC. (*Tokyo*)

For Jenny

Contents

List of Tales Discussed   ix

Introduction, *by William L. Howarth*   1

PART ONE—*View Points*

Harry Levin: Notes from the Underground   24

Stephen L. Mooney: Poe's Detachment   26

Terence Martin: The Imagination at Play   28

Yvor Winters: Edgar Allan Poe: A Crisis in the History of American Obscurantism   30

Joseph M. Garrison, Jr.: The Tales as Poems   32

William Carlos Williams: Edgar Allan Poe   34

PART TWO—*Interpretations*

From Earth to Ether: Poe's Flight into Space, *by Charles O'Donnell*   39

The "Legitimate" Sources of Terror in "The Fall of the House of Usher," *by I. M. Walker*   47

The Dual Hallucination in "The Fall of the House of Usher," *by John S. Hill*   55

Poe's "Ligeia" and the English Romantics, *by Clark Griffith*   63

"Ligeia" and Its Critics: A Plea for Literalism, *by John Lauber*   73

Style and Meaning in "Ligeia" and "William Wilson,"
    by Donald Barlow Stauffer   78

"The Black Cat": Perverseness Reconsidered,
    by James W. Gargano   87

Poe's "The Tell-Tale Heart," by *E. Arthur Robinson*   94

Poe's Detective God, *by Robert Daniel*   103

Chronology of Important Dates   111
Notes on the Editor and Contributors   113
Selected Bibliography   115

List of Tales Discussed

"Angel of the Odd, The," 37
"Assignation, The," 3, 14, 17, 31, 32, 79
"Berenice," 3, 29, 31, 83
"Black Cat, The," 3, 19, 29, 31, 87–93, 101
"BonBon," 37
"Business Man, The," 30
"Cask of Amontillado, The," 2, 28, 115
"Colloquy of Monos and Una, The," 15, 99
"Descent Into the Maelström, A," 17, 18, 97, 98
"Diddling," 35, 37
"Duc d'Omelette," 2
"Eleonora," 15, 31, 74, 101
"Facts in the Case of M. Valdemar, The," 13, 98
"Fall of the House of Usher, The," 3, 8, 10, 15, 17, 20, 25, 32, 47–62, 68, 95, 101, 103, 115
"Gold-Bug, The," 3, 6, 31, 37, 115
"Hop-Frog," 4, 37
"How to Write a Blackwood Article," 5, 7, 17, 63–72
"Imp of the Perverse, The," 27, 101
"King Pest," 7
"Ligeia," 3, 8, 14, 19, 30, 32, 63–86, 101
"Light-House, The," 4
"Loss of Breath," 37
"Man of the Crowd, The," 6
"Man That Was Used Up, The," 37
"Masque of the Red Death, The," 3, 18, 31, 76, 116
"Mellonta Tauta," 6
"Mesmeric Revelation," 13, 98
"Metzengerstein," 2
"Morella," 3, 16, 30, 71, 75
"MS Found in a Bottle," 2, 68
"Murders in the Rue Morgue, The," 3, 22, 31, 37, 79, 103–108

"Mystery of Marie Roget, The," 22, 103, 108
"Narrative of Arthur Gordon Pym, The," 3, 7, 39–46, 97
"Oval Portrait, The," 18
"Philosophy of Furniture, The," 24
"Pit and the Pendulum, The," 2, 19, 95, 97, 115
"Power of Words, The," 16
"Purloined Letter, The," 3, 21, 105, 108
"Rufus Dawes," 36
"Shadow—A Parable," 16
"Silence—A Fable," 13, 31, 63–72
"Slight Predicament, A," 7
"Spectacles, The," 75
"Sphinx, The," 19
"System of Doctor Tarr and Professor Fether, The," 15, 37
"Tell-Tale Heart, The," 3, 11, 17, 19, 31, 94–102
"Unparalleled Adventure of One Hans Pfall, The," 46
"William Wilson," 3, 20, 32, 78–86, 101

Introduction

by William L. Howarth

With almost perfect mistiming, Edgar Allan Poe's *Tales of the Grotesque and Arabesque* first appeared in late November, 1839—just in time for the Christmas trade, when Americans bought nothing but sentimental "gift-books" like *The Token* or *Friendship's Offering*. Poe's two-volume collection of stories, with its odd title and gloomy table of contents, barely survived its inauspicious debut. Anticipating this fate, his brief preface boasted of the book's "unity of design," claimed indifference to "this species of writing," and finally yawned: "It may even happen that, in this manner, I shall never compose anything again." [1] Since he went on to write almost seventy tales, revising many of them two or three times; and since he also wrote several essays and reviews on the art of the story, we can hardly take that preface very seriously. Later he modified its stand, conceding that a tale demands "exercise of the loftiest talent . . . afforded by the wide domains of mere prose," [2] but the phrase *mere prose* betrays his continuing ambivalence. Recognizing the merits of fiction, he still feared that a popular tale was innately vulgar; that only as a poet could he write without "an eye to the paltry compensation, or the more paltry commendation, of mankind" (VII, xlvii).

Money and praise came in paltry amounts to Poe, no matter what he wrote; but as a classic example of posthumous irony, he is famous now largely because of his tales. In fact, who would read him today if he had never written fiction? A few specialists study his poetry and criticism, certainly; while people of all ages and interests read the tales. Practically no other nineteenth century American writer—Mark Twain seems the lone exception—appeals so readily to students, from primary to graduate levels. Even the cultural hucksters live off his fame; we all remember the occasion—a school assembly, a record, or a low-camp

---

[1] *Tales of the Grotesque and Arabesque* (Philadelphia: Lea and Blanchard, 1840), pp. 5–6.

[2] *The Complete Works of Edgar Allan Poe*, ed. James A. Harrison (New York: Thomas Y. Crowell & Co., 1902), XI, 106. Hereafter cited by volume and page number only.

film—when some aging actor first terrified us with "The Cask of Amontillado" or "The Pit and the Pendulum." But the popularity of Poe's tales is also a publisher's delight, as each year copies sell at newsstands, markets, and bookstores to an audience numbering in the millions. In 1970 thirty-seven editions were available, one in its forty-second printing since 1940. If Poe's timing was off a century earlier, perhaps the times themselves were to blame. Yet perhaps he also did not sense the full value of his stories; otherwise he might have seen that their brevity, their sensational events, and their common theme, man's search for identity or self-knowledge, all matched to perfection the story of his life.

Poe's Life

Born in Boston on January 19, 1809, to a pair of itinerant actors, Poe soon fell to the care of Mr. and Mrs. John Allan, a prosperous Richmond couple. The Allans raised him as an unadopted son, without the assurance of a permanent legal—or psychological—identity. Except for a few years abroad, he spent most of his childhood in Virginia, entering the state University at seventeen. In his first year he earned high marks—and some heavy gambling debts. When Allan refused to pay the debts, Poe could not return for a second year. After quarreling with Allan, he ran off to Boston and assumed a new identity. He published his first volume of poems anonymously in 1827, then spent two years in the Army as "Edgar A. Perry." Honorably discharged, he published a second volume in 1829, reconciled briefly with Allan, and enrolled at West Point with his aid. But Allan, whose wife had now died, quickly remarried and left Poe no hope of a legacy. Seeing little future on an officer's pay, he deliberately violated Academy regulations and earned a prompt dismissal. As a parting shot, he used subscriptions from classmates to publish a third volume of poems in 1831.

Having chosen the hazardous identity of professional author, Poe spent his adult life moving among America's literary capitals. From 1831 to 1835 he lived in Baltimore with his aunt and cousin, Maria and Virginia Clemm. He supported this family as a free-lance writer, turning to fiction when poems would not sell. His first tale, a horrific account of castles and curses, appeared in January 1832, as "Metzengerstein." Other early stories, like "Duc d'Omelette," featured satire and cynicism, the literary offspring of his youthful misfortunes. In 1833 he won a story contest with "MS Found in a Bottle," a grim tale of death at sea. One of the contest judges secured Poe an editorship with the *Southern Literary Messenger* in Richmond, a post he held brilliantly from 1835 to 1837. During that time he married his cousin Virginia, a sickly child of fourteen, and developed a taste for alcohol. Both interests taxed his capacities, physical or financial, and added to his mental burdens. Many of his tales during this period—"The Assignation," "Berenice," "Morella"—depict lovers who die to escape earthly troubles and thus preserve their bond of spiritual identity.

Financial troubles brought Poe north again, first to New York and then to Philadelphia, where he settled in 1838. That year he published *The Narrative of Arthur Gordon Pym,* a sensational account of exploration, mutiny, and shipwreck in the South Seas. The book fared poorly, but he was able to sell some shorter pieces, including the important "Ligeia." This tale, an extended study of love, death, and identity, launched the major period of Poe's story-writing career. In Philadelphia he returned to editing, first with *Burton's Gentleman's Magazine* and then with the more popular monthly, *Graham's Magazine.* Besides reviews and essays, he contributed important tales—"The Fall of the House of Usher," "William Wilson," "The Masque of the Red Death," "The Murders of the Rue Morgue"—in which the theme of identity took on darker tones, reflecting his interest in problems of mental aberration. He resigned from *Graham's* in 1842, tried unsuccessfully to start a new journal, then free-lanced for two years, writing some of his most famous tales—"The Tell-Tale Heart," "The Black Cat," "The Gold Bug," "The Purloined Letter." In these stories, the oscillation of a narrator's identity—from psychotic alienation to rational control—seems close to Poe's situation at that time. Although his creative powers were at their height, his wife was dying of tuberculosis, his alcoholism had become acute, and money was in short supply.

In 1844 Poe returned to New York, where he worked on a newspaper before joining the weekly *Broadway Journal.* With publication of "The Raven" in 1845 he began to be recognized; his series of unflattering critiques, *The Literati,* soon made him notorious. He wrote fewer tales during this period, but several reviews, especially those on Hawthorne, set forth his ideas on fiction. For a while he was sole owner of the *Journal,* until poor financial judgment led to its failure in January 1846. His literary feuding provoked a fist fight and a libel suit, both of which he won; but these incidents dashed the reputation he might have enjoyed. After years of decline, Virginia died during the harsh winter of 1847; and from that point on, drinking and poverty steadily ruined Poe's own health. His life became chaotic: attacks of delirium, suicide attempts, and a series of romantic entanglements followed in dizzying succession. Yet chaos often inspires the artist; in 1848 he completed *Eureka,* an ambitious philosophical essay that depicts man's ascension to "an identity with God." Several times he planned marriage or vowed temperance, only to see his hopes collapse. His last published story, "Hop-Frog," in which a dwarf triumphs over a lifetime of torment, echoes Poe's deepest needs. While traveling from Richmond to New York, he disappeared into Baltimore for five days. When found, he was semi-conscious and beyond recovery; he died on October 7, 1849. Among his papers was an unfinished tale about a writer who seeks isolation, only to collapse from self-induced hysteria.[3] This fragment is Poe's last statement on the problem of identity: We are all alone, and yet we all need each other. The history of his reputation illustrates that theme; once notorious and discredited, he is recognized today as a founder of modern psychological fiction. His followers have rarely agreed on his merits—Fyodor Dostoyevsky (pro) and Henry James (con) are the classic disputants—but they have never disputed his influence.

Poe and the Romantic Age

Poe apparently sought no influence as a writer; in a famous lecture he branded as "the heresy of *The Didactic*" the belief that literature should instruct, charging that ". . . We Americans especially have patronized this happy idea; and we Bostonians, very especially, have developed it in full" (XIV, 211). Statements like these earned him the lasting title of iconoclast, but we should note that his attack on dogma is dogmatic itself. Much of his criticism instructs, usually by flailing contemporary values, while several of his tales satirize current events.[4] As Terence Martin* remarks, Poe simply rejected conventional pieties and championed instead all that was abnormal and bizarre. When it came to the heresy of didacticism, apparently the arch-heretic was Poe himself!

Since he was inconsistent about the relation of art to ideas, we should not be surprised to learn that Poe's tales are closely tied to nineteenth-century American culture, especially to that period, roughly between 1830 and 1865, which historians now call "The Romantic Age" of American literature. During those years, stretching from the presidency of Andrew Jackson to the end of the Civil War, the nation expanded to the west and divided north from south. In politics it was an age of growth and conflict, triumph and ordeal; in literature it was America's first period of major artists. New England developed into a

---

* Hereafter, this symbol will indicate that the author's essay appears in this volume.

[3] "The Light-House," ed. T. O. Mabbot, *Notes and Queries* CLXXXII (April 25, 1942), 226–27.

[4] Walter Taylor Fuller, "Israfel in Motley," *Sewanee Review* XLII (1934), 330–40.

great center of literary activity, largely through the work of Emerson, Holmes, Longfellow, and Lowell. Most of these men became "Romantics" by absorbing intellectual doctrine from abroad. They read German philosophers, British poets, and French social theorists; out of this material they fashioned a buoyant liberal creed. Above all, they were optimists: they believed in man's integrity, in nature's beneficence, in the efficacy of social and political reform. But there were writers outside this New England group—"outside" either by residence or temperament—who took a darker view of the issues. They assumed that man was often fallible, that nature was indifferent or even hostile to his fate, that "progress" was just another of his empty dreams. The most prominent of these dissenters were Nathaniel Hawthorne, Herman Melville—and Edgar Allan Poe.

We should not assume that Poe categorically rejected the major authors, but it is true that he attacked them frequently and bitterly. He accused Emerson of obscurity, scoffed at his "mystics for mysticism's sake" (XV, 260), and repeatedly assailed *The Dial,* a journal that Emerson founded and edited. Concluding an essay on Hawthorne's tales, he sarcastically warned of Yankee contagion:

> Let him mend his pen, get a bottle of visible ink, come out from the Old Manse, cut Mr. Alcott, hang (if possible) the editor of "The Dial," and throw out of the window to the pigs all his odd numbers of 'The North American Review.' (XIII, 155)

Each allusion in this sentence snipes at the New England Establishment: the Old Manse was formerly Emerson's home in Concord, Massachusetts; Bronson Alcott, the father of Louisa May Alcott, was Emerson's close friend; and the *North American Review,* later edited by James Russell Lowell, was Boston's most prominent monthly journal.

Despite the rancor of Poe's charges, their substance is not impressive. Most of his objections were simply a matter of taste. Some New Englanders wrote prose that seemed to him too cloudy and ambiguous. Spoofing their excesses, he found that "the tone transcendental"

> . . . consists in seeing into the nature of affairs a very great deal farther than anybody else. This second sight is very efficient when properly managed. A little reading of the *Dial* will carry you a great way. Eschew, in this case, big words; get them as small as possible, and write them upside down. (II, 276)

As for genuine differences of opinion, most of them sprang from the fact that he was beyond the New England circle. He once professed allegiance to his birthplace, signing his first book of poems "By a Bostonian"; but a Southern heritage claimed most of his loyalty. Politically, he accepted the conservative ideal of States' rights in an agrarian republic, thus directly opposing the views of a liberal and industrial North. An urban man all his life, he nevertheless attacked the "huge, smoking cities" for their destruction of the old America: "Green leaves shrank before the hot breath of furnaces. The fair face of Nature was deformed as with the ravages of some loathsome disease" (IV, 203). Cities created new political institutions, like centralized government and universal suffrage, that spread the influence of Jacksonian democracy—in the conservative vocabulary, "mob rule." To Poe this spectre meant the end of individual liberty. In an early tale, "The Man of the Crowd," he presents an anatomy of the urban masses, comparing inequities in "the crowd" with madness in "the man" who walks the city streets for no apparent reason. In "Mellonta Tauta," a satirical glimpse of the future, he forecasts the end of equal representation, concluding: "democracy is a very admirable form of government—for dogs" (VI, 209).

Poe's political conservatism seems to separate him from the New Englanders, but their differences were actually modest. True, he violently disagreed with the Abolitionists. A conventional attitude toward slavery accounts for his crude portraits of Negro characters. The stereotyped speech and shuffling manner of Jupiter, a figure in "The Gold-Bug," are insulting to modern readers, white or black. On the other hand, his contempt for cities matches the attitudes that in New England inspired the founding of Brook Farm and Thoreau's retreat to Walden Pond. As for Poe's distrust of "the Mob," more than one Northern liberal also worried about the fate of individual freedom. Two protests against the Mexican-American war, Thoreau's "Civil Disobedience" and Lowell's "The Biglow Papers," called for resistance to majority rule. Even Emerson, a life-long proponent of democracy, once complained to his Journal of "the unmixed malignity, the withering selfishness, the impudent vulgarity" of an open political meeting.[5] Poe's differences with established opinion, then, were matters of emphasis rather than principle. Taking up literary issues, we find even more connections between him and his supposed antagonists.

Poe's Tales: Practice and Theory

In dealing with Poe's career, critics often speak first of his literary "theory" and then of his "practice." The two complement each other

[5] *Journals of Ralph Waldo Emerson,* eds. E. W. Emerson and W. E. Forbes (Boston: Houghton Mifflin Company, 1910), III, 405.

closely, but not because they developed in that order. The confusion stems from Poe's famous essay, "The Philosophy of Composition," which claims he wrote "The Raven" according to strict, predetermined rules. In actuality, his theories grew out of his poems and tales, and not the other way around. By making the theories fit the works, he simply described what he had formerly implied. Since his "theory" came mostly after the fact, we had best begin with a brief description of his "practice." In the relatively short space of seventeen years, 1832 to 1849, he published sixty-eight tales, which we may divide into three categories—"grotesque," "arabesque," and "ratiocinative"—corresponding roughly to the early, middle, and late periods of his brief career.

The grotesques, written mostly between 1832 and 1837, were primarily apprentice work. During that period Poe learned to write fiction by parodying the type of "sensational" story that had become popular in British and American journals. A fair example of this type is "King Pest," published in 1835. Two drunks break into a series of London shops and accidentally encounter a strange gathering at an undertaker's. Poe's description of one young lady illustrates his flair for the absurd:

> An air of extreme *haut ton,* however, pervaded her whole appearance; she wore in a graceful and *degagé* manner, a large and beautiful winding-sheet of the finest India lawn; her hair hung in ringlets over her neck; a soft smile played about her mouth; but her nose, extremely long, thin, sinuous, flexible, and pimpled, hung down far below her under-lip, and, in spite of the delicate manner in which she now and then moved it to one side or the other with her tongue, gave to her countenance a somewhat equivocal expression. (II, 176)

His triumph in this vein is a pair of tales entitled "How to Write a Blackwood Article" and "A Slight Predicament." In the first tale, already quoted for its parody of Yankee style, an editor advises Miss Psyche Zenobia to "pay minute attention to the sensations" (II, 274). Consequently, the second tale is her account of her own decapitation! While these stories are witty and often amusing, they are not Poe's best work, and essays on them do not appear in this volume.[6]

The earliest—and longest—tale discussed here is *The Narrative of Arthur Gordon Pym.* Often called a "novel" because of its length, *Pym*

---

[6] See Edward H. Davidson, "The Short Story as Grotesque" in *Poe: A Critical Study* (Cambridge, Mass.: Harvard University Press, 1957), pp. 136–55; Stephen L. Mooney, "The Comic in Poe's Fiction," *American Literature* XXXIII (1962), 433–41; and James Southall Wilson, "The Devil Was In It," *The American Mercury* XXIV (1931), 215–20.

seems closer in form and content to what Poe termed a "romance," that is, a nonpoetic narrative ". . . having for its object . . . a *definite* pleasure . . . presenting perceptible images with definite . . . sensations" (VII, xliii). Although Poe based the tale on actual accounts of Pacific voyages, he added plenty of "definite sensations"—mutiny, shipwreck, cannibalism—and a scheme of "perceptible images" that anticipates Melville's color symbolism in *Moby Dick*.[7] Charles O'Donnell * notes that the tale appeared at a significant point in Poe's career. Coming after the grotesques, it was his first attempt to write a serious story about man's frailty and fate, two themes that dominated his later works.

Poe's most famous tales, and therefore those most discussed in this volume, are the "arabesques" he wrote between 1838 and 1844. He used the term *arabesque* for tales that were fanciful in tone but sombre in meaning—possibly in tribute to the *Arabian Nights,* which may have inspired his bizarre characters, unified plots, and flowing narrative style.[8] Like the Arabian tales, told by a princess to postpone her execution, Poe's arabesques are serious entertainments; for in their scarifying subjects of murder, graves, and ghosts, the careful reader finds intriguing psychological dimensions. Tales like "Ligeia" or "The Fall of the House of Usher" fascinate us because Poe has deliberately mixed their natural and supernatural events to pose a difficult riddle: Are we haunted in this world, or do we haunt ourselves?

The somewhat later "ratiocinative" tales, written between 1841 and 1845, have not yet received the attention they merit. The ratiocinative hero is an intriguing mixture of sense and sensibility, reason and imagination. Faced with a difficult crime or puzzle, he swiftly unlocks the mystery with a series of brilliant deductions. These tales are forerunners of modern "detective" fiction, but with an important difference: the absence of suspense. The hero often reveals his solution at once, then gives a lengthy explanation of his reasoning. Poe's appeal is rational, not emotional; he provides buried treasure or a mutilated corpse to liven the logic a bit, but the stories are clearly more than ingenious puzzles—they may even represent his last effort to popularize certain ideas about the human mind. Preceding his final essays—"The Philosophy of Composition," "The Poetic Principle," and *Eureka*—by only a few years, the ratiocinative tales are probably the point at which practice began to become theory.

Comparing the two realms is difficult in Poe's case, because they differed so widely: his ideas were mystical and speculative, his methods

---

[7] Davidson, pp. 156–80. Sidney Kaplan, "An Introduction to Pym," reprinted in *Poe: A Collection of Critical Essays,* ed. Robert Regan (Englewood Cliffs, N.J.: Prentice-Hall, Inc., 1967), pp. 145–163. Hereafter cited as *TCV,* by page number.

[8] L. Moffitt Cecil, "Poe's 'Arabesque,' " *Comparative Literature* XVIII (1966), 55–70.

practical and systematic. In literary theory he echoed the views of Emerson and the New Englanders, and like them he took many ideas from Coleridge, the English poet and critic. Since Coleridge borrowed from Plato, we could call Poe's theories "neo-Platonic." But in literary practice he resembled certain eighteenth-century authors, such as Joseph Addison or Alexander Pope, who supposedly wrote according to "rules" and delighted in order above all else. A major influence on these writers was Aristotle, whose *Poetics* is a model of the rational, systematic approach to literature. Somewhere between these extremes we find Poe, assuming he is perfectly consistent:

> . . . Theory and practice are in so much *one*, that the former implies or includes the latter. A theory is only good as such, in proportion to its reducibility to practice. If the practice fail, it is because the theory is imperfect. (XI, 39)

A "reducible" consistency characterizes Poe's general thoughts on literature. Following Coleridge and Plato, he held that literary genres express man's highest ideals: poetry is Beauty, prose is Truth, and a combination of these two, whether in drama, essay, or tale, approaches Goodness—the most elusive of ideals. To this Platonic view of literature's *ends* Poe attached an Aristotelian idea of its *means*. Unlike Coleridge, he believed that formal or technical devices—plot, character, style —are just as important to a writer as lofty ideals. In his view, literature best expresses its ideals *effectively*; by means of suggestive strategems, or *effects*, rather than overt statements. A writer cannot afford to sacrifice technique for the sake of doctrine; he is obliged to remain free of extraneous influence and personal bias. Obviously, this view places a high premium on the artifice of literature, on the fact that it is quite apart from day to day life.

Many of Poe's ideas on literature are interesting, but only those relevant to his fiction merit close attention here. His belief in the Truth of prose raises special problems concerning his tales. In *Eureka*, Poe defined his idea of an ultimate form of Truth:

> A thing is consistent in the ratio of its truth—true in the ratio of its consistency. *A perfect consistency, I repeat, can be nothing but an absolute truth.* (XVI, 302)

Joseph Garrison* explains that Poe's concept of Truth was dualistic, embracing both the surface and interior of things. The "perfect consistency" of which he spoke therefore contained opposite as well as homogeneous parts. To Poe, a tale was truthful not only when its characters behaved habitually, but also when they met in habitual conflict. Conflict could only be carried so far, however.

. . . although the representation of no human character should be quar-
relled with for its inconsistency, we yet require that the inconsistencies be
not absolute antagonisms to the extent of neutralization: they may be
permitted to be oils and waters, but they must not be alkalis and acids.
(XII, 51)

This is good rhetoric, but it solves few of our problems. The differences of critical opinion in this volume indicate that Poe's "perfect
consistency" is still not perfectly accessible. Against the critics' dissent,
however, we might set his statement, ". . . every work of art should
contain *within itself* all that is requisite for its own comprehension"
(XI, 78; italics supplied). Many disputes over his tales stem from the
use of outside information—history, psychology, even theology—to explain the author rather than his works. Claiming that Roderick and
Madeline reflect Poe's fear of incest [9] answers no literary questions
about "The Fall of the House of Usher." To understand the work itself
we must put aside Poe's unconscious mind and focus on his conscious
handling of characters. By studying material *within* the tales, we may
more readily grasp the Truth, or "perfect consistency," that he believed
they expressed.

The Method of Poe's Tales

As a critic, Poe stressed matters of form while his contemporaries
worried about content. He believed that method supports meaning,
that we must know *how* literature works before we can fully understand
what it says. We can test this standard by examining the major aspects
of Poe's narrative technique—structure, character, style, and mode—
before taking up the question of his fictional "Truth."

Structure, a planned framework, is the essential element in Poe's
tales; his review of Hawthorne's *Twice-Told Tales* explains just why:
"In the whole composition there should be no word written, of which
the tendency, direct or indirect, is not to the one pre-established design" (XI, 108). The important word is "pre-established." Aristotle
noted that literary action has a three-part structure, beginning, middle,
and end; Poe liked to add that beginning and end should not forget
each other. Furthermore, the intervening action should constitute a
unified pattern, *"in which no part can be displaced without ruin to the
whole"* (X, 117). As we might expect, his own tales reflect this concern.

[9] Marie Bonaparte, *The Life and Works of Edgar Allan Poe: A Psycho-Analytic
Interpretation,* trans. John Rodker (London: Imago Publishing Company, Ltd.,
1949), p. 232.

Each event forms a link in the unbroken chain of plot: beginning posits end; middle connects both; end fulfills beginning.

Consider, for example, how the structure of "The Tell-Tale Heart" develops from its narrator's opening remark, "The disease had sharpened my senses . . . Above all was the sense of hearing acute." As he plots a murder, his hearing becomes even more acute. He hears his victim groan: "I knew the sound well. Many a night . . . it has welled up from my own bosom, deepening, with its dreadful echo, the terrors that distracted me." Just before the murder, he hears a beating heart. The beat quickens with his excitement, pounds in frenzy as he kills, and thumps heavily long after his victim is dead. After concealing the body carefully, he finds police officers at the door. A neighbor, whose hearing must also be acute, has reported a suspicious sound—the victim's final shriek. The narrator calmly shows the police around, bids them rest near the very spot of concealment, and then begins to hear a beating heart. The sound increases with his own agitation, but the police cannot hear it. At length, tormented by the pounding noise, he shrieks, "I admit the deed!—tear up the plank!—here!—it is the beating of his hideous heart!" (V, 88–94). When we compare this ending with the tale's beginning, however, we recognize that all along the narrator has been hearing only *his own heart*. Details in the tale's middle—the groan, the heartbeat, the neighbor—then become meaningful, until even its title has a new significance: the "tell-tale" heart belongs to him who tells this tale!

In grasping the ironic "point" here, we encounter Poe's most characteristic objective in story-telling: *effect.* He meant by this term the psychological impact a story makes upon its readers. In a short tale the impact can be quite strong, since "brevity is in direct ratio [to] the intensity of the intended effect" (XIV, 197). Poe often spoke of effect as something "unique and single," but he recognized that it consists of several psychological factors, emotional, rational, even spiritual in nature. Our responses to a tale may therefore vary, but they all arise from one general effect. No tale presents only one idea; as he explained, ". . . how one idea can be 'gradually unfolded' without other ideas, is, to us, a mystery of mysteries" (XI, 83).

Some critics have objected to Poe's idea of effect, believing that he meant by it some sort of contrived riddle.[10] Sometimes, he does seem to think stories are designed to fool the unsuspecting or literal-minded reader. Commenting on Hawthorne's tales, he asserts that the "true import" of "The Minister's Black Veil" has to do with a young woman

[10] Cleanth Brooks and Robert Penn Warren, *Understanding Fiction* (New York: F. S. Crofts and Co., 1943), pp. 202–5.

and "a crime of dark dye." This would seem to justify Yvor Winters' *
charge that Poe is an American "obscurantist." On the other hand, it
would be unfair to accuse Poe of simply playing games with his audience. As he noted, an effect must provoke responses: ". . . the writer
who aims at impressing the people . . . is *always* wrong when he fails
in forcing [them] to receive the impression" (XIII, 149). In turn, their
responses should form an orderly sequence, reflecting the tale's structural unity and the harmony of its communicants:

> During the hour of perusal the soul of the reader is at the writer's control.
> . . . They two, together, have created this thing. Henceforward there is a
> bond of sympathy between them, a sympathy which irradiates every sub-
> sequent page of the book. (XIII, 146, 153)

If structure was Poe's primary concern in fiction, characterization was
surely his second. Like other story writers, he had to invent characters
who could think, act, or tell his tales believably. But on this score the
critics have always found him inadequate. They have called his characters flat, undeveloped, and a poor contrast to those of Charles Dickens,
his famous contemporary. Poe himself objected to flat characters, especially to moral stereotypes: "The characters have no *character* . . . no
attempt seems to have been made at individualization. All the good
ladies and gentlemen are demi-gods and demi-goddesses, and all the
bad are—the d ——l" (VIII, 60). Yet next to Dickens' characters, Poe's
still look like caricatures. Demi-gods of another variety, they are unfail-
ingly hypersensitive, melancholy, or mad. Often we do not know their
pasts, their surroundings, or even their names. The women all seem
willowy and wasted; the men often languish in irredeemable despair.

Some of these defects we might attribute to Poe's literary training.
He prepared for fiction by writing poetry, the one form of Romantic
literature that portrays few characters in depth. When he characterizes
with *poetic* devices, his efforts reflect the merits and defects of the Romantic mode. His favorite strategy, description, employs the vivid
imagery familiar to his poems:

> She stood alone. Her small, bare, and silvery feet gleamed in the black
> mirror of marble beneath her. Her hair, not as yet more than half
> loosened for the night from its ball-room array, clustered, amid a shower
> of diamonds, round and round her classical head, in curls like those of
> the young hyacinth. A snowy-white and gauze-like drapery seemed to be
> nearly the sole covering to her delicate form. . . . (II, 111)

While this may draw an impressive portrait of the lady, it suggests no
depths. The lady does not become a dramatic human being; she is har-
monious but static; unable to laugh, gossip, or fly into a tantrum.

Merely the outline of a person, she is still very much what Poe intended:

> . . . it is curious to observe how very slight a degree of truth is sufficient to satisfy the mind, which acquiesces in the absence of numerous essentials in the thing depicted. An outline frequently stirs the spirit more pleasantly than the most elaborate picture. (XI, 84)

Though disapproving of Poe's characters, many critics have commented favorably on his handling of narrators. The fact that most of the tales are told in retrospect by a first-person voice raises certain questions. Does the pronoun "I" indicate that Poe is narrating, or is the "I" an imaginary character? Narrating in retrospect, he knows the end of the tale as he begins it; how can he create suspense without fraud? And if what he tells is only what he has seen and understood, why should we accept it as reliable, especially if he gives any evidence of being mad? Poe recognizes these difficulties but delights in not resolving them. In several tales, he deliberately mocks the convention of the first-person narrator. Miss Zenobia continues to chatter after losing her head, "I will candidly confess that my feelings were now of the most singular—nay, of the most mysterious, the most perplexing, and incomprehensible character" (II, 293). In a more serious vein, narrators like the angels Eiros and Monos or the mesmerized Vankirk and Valdemar speak—from beyond the grave—about the nature of death. In any of these tales the message seems clear, but what are we to make of its medium?

First, we must understand that the narrators are *personae*, imaginary characters shaped for the tales in which they appear. Poe understood the concept of persona, as is clear from these remarks:

> In all commentating upon Shakespeare, there has been a radical error, never yet mentioned. It is the error of attempting to expound his characters—to account for their actions—to reconcile his inconsistencies—not as if they were the coinage of a human brain, but as if they had been actual existences upon earth. We talk of Hamlet the man, instead of Hamlet the *dramatis persona*—of Hamlet that God, in place of Hamlet that Shakespeare created. (XII, 226–7)

Discussing this matter at length, James Gargano clearly establishes that Poe must not be confused with his fictive world [11]—a point also made by Stephen Mooney.* The issue is not quite dead, for interpretations still appear in which a character's thoughts or deeds are taken to be Poe's.

---

[11] "The Question of Poe's Narrators," *College English* XXV (1963), 177–81. Reprinted in *TCV*, pp. 164–71.

Next, we must agree that our job as readers is to determine the reliability of the narrators. If we cannot accept them as Poe's mouthpieces, how shall we evaluate what they say? The narrators themselves do not help us. They confess to poor memories, to ignorance, even to deliberate exaggeration. The nostalgic, sentimental narrator of "The Assignation" is a typical example:

> It was at Venice, beneath the covered archway there called the *Ponte di Sospiri*, that I met for the third or fourth time the person of whom I speak. It is with a confused recollection that I bring to mind the circumstances of that meeting. Yet I remember—ah! how should I forget?—the deep midnight, the Bridge of Sighs, the beauty of woman, and the Genius of Romance that stalked up and down the narrow canal. . . .
> —Who does not remember that, at such a time as this, the eye, like a shattered mirror, multiplies the images of its sorrow, and sees in innumerable far off places, the woe which is close at hand? (II, 110)

If this speaker were on a witness stand, his testimony would be difficult for a jury to accept. The "Genius of Romance" colors his memories, permitting him to recall a suggestive name but to forget an exact number. He cannot remember circumstances, only "atmosphere." Finally, he admits that grief may have distorted his senses, both then and now. The eye cannot be trusted, he tells us; we must wonder if the "I" is any better!

Many critics simply dismiss these witnesses as totally unreliable. The narrator of "Ligeia," for example, has been accused of telling a story that never actually occurred. Grief-stricken at the death of Ligeia, a woman of dark beauty, passion, and invincible will, he marries her exact opposite, the fair, placid, and retiring Rowena. Still haunted by his memories of Ligeia, he neglects Rowena until she suddenly and mysteriously dies. During his long deathwatch a strange transformation occurs in her body; the color returns; the limbs stir; eventually the lady rises. When the shroud falls from her face, he sees not Rowena, but Ligeia restored to life! (II, 248–68). The narrator obviously believes his story, but some readers assume it is utter fantasy—a macabre form of wish-fulfillment. His account is unreliable, they contend, because it is extremely subjective. Besides admitting to a poor memory, he describes events as "visions" and "ideas," as things that happen mostly in his mind. Although he may want to tell a credible story, the argument runs, he unknowingly tells quite another.[12]

But even if this description is accurate, it still does not entirely discredit the narrator. Since he is our only source of information, we

---

[12] Roy P. Basler, "The Interpretation of 'Ligeia'," *College English* V (1944), 363–72. Reprinted in *TCV*, pp. 51–63.

must rely on his words even to prove that they are unreliable. Oddly enough, we must believe him when he says that Ligeia dies in order to disbelieve his account of her return. Poe has thus fitted us with a neat and insoluble paradox: either we believe everything his narrator tells us, or we believe nothing; in either case we are left with an impossible story—one about a "true" ghost, or one about a "false" teller! We might also apply this reasoning to "The Fall of the House of Usher." At the end of that tale, the narrator sees and hears a woman who has been dead for several days. If he hallucinated the experience, his narrative is equally hallucinatory. Moreover, if we distrust the end of his story, we have no basis for believing *any* of it. We cannot, as we do in life, call some statements true and others false. In life we draw information from a variety of sources, but in Poe's tales we must rely on a single point of view.

Complicating the issue of reliability is another problem, the narrator's state of mind. In several tales, narrators betray derangement— usually by denying they are mad. Obsessed with proving their sanity, they tell stories that become elaborate acts of self-defense. We cannot ignore their rationalizations, but we cannot object to them without repudiating part of each tale's design. Arguing that a madman could not tell "Ligeia" so coherently is also invalid,[13] since coherence is not an infallible sign of sanity. Some forms of madness, like paranoia, appear to be quite logical and orderly—up to a point. Poe long contended that order is but the simplest product of human reason. Carried to an extreme form, it becomes monomania, the fixation upon a single desire.

None are more orderly than those narrators who explain their madness to us. The narrator of "Eleonora," questioning "whether madness is or is not the loftiest intelligence," recognizes two phases in his mental history: the past, of which his memory is clear and trustworthy, and the present, a period of "shadow and doubt":

> Therefore, what I shall tell of the earlier period, believe; and to what I may relate of the later time, give only such credit as may seem due; or doubt it altogether . . . (IV, 236–7)

What he asks is quite impossible, because the only point from which he can view the past is the present. His present mental troubles, then, inevitably affect his image of the past. Yet even so, Poe has made his point: the line between sanity and insanity is unclear. A sane man may play mad, a madman may feign sanity; a paradox illustrated in "The System of Doctor Tarr and Professor Fether" as a madman observes:

[13] James Schroeter, "A Misreading of Poe's 'Ligeia'," *PMLA* LXXVI (1961), 397–406.

[A lunatic's] cunning . . . is proverbial, and great. If he has a project in view, he conceals his design with a marvellous wisdom; and the dexterity with which he counterfeits sanity, presents, to the metaphysician, one of the most singular problems in the study of mind. When a madman appears *thoroughly* sane, indeed, it is high time to put him in a strait-jacket. (VI, 72)

The problem of a narrator's reliability or sanity may seem too difficult to resolve, but E. Arthur Robinson* and James Gargano* offer one answer: *moral simplicity* in the narrators may reflect their mental instability. When Poe's narrator speaks too constantly in his own defense, when he ignores evidence that might contradict him, then we should mark him down for cautious observation. In a sense, he is a victim of didacticism, that form of moral simplicity Poe found in Longfellow:

His invention, his imagery, his all, is made subservient to the elucidation of some one or more points (but rarely of more than one) which he looks upon as truth. (XI, 69)

The remaining aspects of Poe's fictional technique, style and mode, are closely related. Style, the arrangement of words, was obviously important to him. Observing, in a sketch entitled "The Power of Words," that words are the sole agent of thought (VI, 143), he intended always to choose his language carefully. But his style is far from perfect. At its worst it suffers from an affected vocabulary and pretentious allusions. The death scene in "Morella" illustrates how these faults may create a lugubrious effect rather than the intended pathos:

. . . thy days shall be days of sorrow—that sorrow which is the most lasting of impressions, as the cypress is the most enduring of trees. For the hours of thy happiness are over; and joy is not gathered twice in a life, as the roses of Paestum twice in a year. Thou shalt no longer, then, play the Teian with time, but, being ignorant of the myrtle and the vine, thou shalt bear about with thee thy shroud of the earth, as do the Moslemin [sic] at Mecca. (II, 30–1)

Only the story's serious theme allays our suspicion of stylistic parody, one of Poe's frequent resources. Happily, the preceding example is not typical of his writing. In fact, it is hard to characterize his "typical" style, for at his best he could fit words, as Donald Stauffer* notes, to any tale's design.

His comic style has already been noted, in a passage from "King Pest" (see page 7). There, deliberate shifts between levels of diction, from the elegant *degagé* to the ugly *pimpled,* underscore the absurdity of his description. In a more serious vein, he could adopt a scriptural style for a tale such as "Shadow: a Parable":

> And lo! from among those sable draperies where the sounds of song de-
> parted, there came forth a dark and undefined shadow—a shadow such
> as the moon, when low in heaven, might fashion from the figure of a man:
> but it was the shadow neither of man, nor of God, nor of any familiar
> thing. (II, 149)

Devices drawn from the King James Bible—the conjunction *and* in an
initial position, the inverted *came forth . . . a shadow,* the negative
series *neither . . . nor . . . nor*—create an effect of solemnity and
dignity that matches Poe's somber discussion of death. Other varieties
of his style appear in previous quotations: a "musical" style, in which
prose sounds like poetry ("The Assignation," p. 14); a "natural" style,
with a clear and unaffected tone ("How to Write a Blackwood Article,"
p. 5); and a "sensational" style, in which strong rhythms dominate
("The Tell-Tale Heart," p. 99). Working together, as in this passage
from "A Descent into the Maelström," the elements of sound, sense, and
stress can evoke a powerful effect:

> Here the vast bed of the waters, seamed and scarred into a thousand con-
> flicting channels, burst suddenly into phrensied convulsion—heaving,
> boiling, hissing—gyrating in gigantic and innumerable vortices, and all
> whirling and plunging on to the eastward with a rapidity which water
> never elsewhere assumes, except in precipitous descents. (II, 228)

The mode of Poe's tales is as variable, and sometimes as inclusive, as
their style. In order to interpret his stories, we have to have some idea
of their objectives. In the early grotesques, his use of exaggerated plots,
characters, and language to criticize human follies indicates that the
mode is *satire.* In the arabesque tales, the mode is *allegory.* Descriptions
of settings, characters, and events indicate that this fictive world represents something larger than itself, as in the opening description of the
House of Usher, where "bleak walls . . . vacant eye-like windows . . .
rank sedges . . . decayed trees . . . black and lurid tarn . . ." (III,
274) all represent the struggle between life and death, creation and
destruction, that will follow. The mode of the ratiocinative tales is
somewhat more difficult to define; perhaps it is best called *documen-
tary.* Poe's master "detectives" document events in order to locate their
place in time—they try to learn what has happened, is happening, will
happen. He therefore constructs stories which imitate the consistency
of actual life: the plots follow strict cause and effect, the characters
behave moderately, and they speak in a straightforward style. In sum,
we can say that during his career Poe's fictional objective moved from
criticism (satire) to speculation (allegory) and finally to analysis (docu-
mentary). Apparently it was Truth, everchanging yet always the object
of his quest, that moved him to speak in these various modes; and it is
therefore to "Truth" that we must now turn.

The Meaning of Poe's Tales

Every reader of Poe eventually faces the same question: in view of his anti-didacticism, what can his tales mean? Are they supposed to convey an experience, a lesson, some particular sort of knowledge, or are they told just for the sake of telling? In "The Poetic Principle" Poe claimed "there neither exists nor *can* exist any work more thoroughly dignified . . . [than] this poem which is a poem and nothing more—this poem written solely for the poem's sake" (XIV, 272). Such statements would seem to preclude other motives; they have provoked many critics to charge him with "amorality." Yet as we have already noted, Poe tampered not with the ends of prose, only with its means. What sort of meaning, then, emerges as his "Truth"?

As we have also noted, Poe only grudgingly participated in the cultural movement known as Romanticism. Some of its attitudes he adopted; others he resisted or treated equivocally. In his criticism, for example, he says the artistic imagination is man's noblest faculty; yet in "The Oval Portrait" an artist destroys a woman by painting her perfect likeness. Toward other elements of the Romantic philosophy, he was equally ambivalent. To most orthodox Romantics, oceans, mountains, or forests were symbols the mind could read and understand, and Nature was only meaningful as it reflected that mind. Emerson illustrates this idea in his brief poem, "The Rhodora." Recalling a flower found deep in the woods, he asks why such beauty should grace that lonely spot. His answer, "The self-same Power that brought me there brought you," [14] means that the flower helped him express an idea of beauty, that he helped the flower become beautiful. Emerson's poem depicts *correspondence*, a Romantic term for the psychological experience that fuses mind and matter, subject and object, into a collective whole, "the self-same Power." This belief, that life could be something grand and coherent, encouraged most Romantics to celebrate Nature, human perception, and the Self—all themes that Poe opposed, although he accepted the principle of correspondence.

In the first place, he could not agree to a positive view of Nature. Nature seldom appears in his tales, but when it does it resists man's understanding. The "Red Death," the black cat, and the Maelström are not parables, but riddles; they deny Nature's role in a cooperative universe. That giant whirlpool in the North Sea, relentlessly drawing men

[14] *The Complete Works of Ralph Waldo Emerson,* ed. E. W. Emerson (Boston: Houghton Mifflin Company, 1904) IX, 38.

and boats to certain destruction, resembles Melville's world more than Emerson's; for Poe's sailor—like Ishmael—escapes death only by an odd quirk of fate. Seemingly tumultuous, the Maelström is far more orderly than man; it runs in daily cycles that he must learn to obey. A misread watch leads him into the whirlpool; some chance observations allow him to live until it subsides. But the story celebrates neither man's ingenuity nor Nature's beneficence. The Maelström emerges from this conflict an awesome, enigmatic force, while the sailor is a shattered husk:

You suppose me a *very* old man—but I am not. It took less than a single day to change these hairs from a jetty black to white, to weaken my limbs, and to unstring my nerves, so that I tremble at the least exertion, and am frightened at a shadow. (II, 225)

Secondly, though Poe accepted the importance of human perception, he had little faith in human judgment. Too often man's senses bow to his fallible imagination: "Ill-fated and mysterious man!—bewildered in the brilliancy of thine own imagination, and fallen in the flames of thine own youth!" (II, 109). Working in tandem, imagination and the senses easily distort situations, as in "The Pit and the Pendulum." Placed in a dark pit, given little to perceive, the narrator soon falls into unreasoning despair. Imagination torments him far more than his captors, and his ultimate rescue lies in the hands of others (V, 67–87). Misperception also occurs in broad daylight, as Poe demonstrates in "The Sphinx." The narrator, dreading some "fearful intelligence" about a plague, creates fearful omens with his own intelligence. Two glimpses of a huge "creature" on a distant hill convince him that he is either mad or dying; closer examination reveals a tiny insect on the window pane, "about the sixteenth of an inch distant from the pupil of my eye" (VI, 244).

Finally, Poe agreed with Romantics that the Self assigns meaning to the world, but he preferred to dramatize the unfortunate consequences of this act. Several of his narrators go well beyond correspondence, forcing upon other people or objects the burden of their own twisted desires. The "identity" they assume with others yields not understanding, but brutal self-gratification. Poe often exposes this corruption by punning on the words *eye* and *I*. The narrator of "The Tell-Tale Heart" kills because he hates not the victim but his "Evil Eye"; in "The Black Cat" he punishes the "evil" in a pet by cutting out "one of its eyes"; in "Ligeia" he brings a woman back to "life" by dwelling upon his memory of her "full . . . black . . . and . . . wild eyes" (V, 89, 145; II, 268). In each of these tales, the "I" only imagines "evil" or "life"; the "eyes" passively reflect his perverse will. By making the narrators blind to their mistakes, Poe criticizes the Self's tendency to impose upon the world.

That is the bent of Roderick Usher's melancholy friend, whose story is purely self-serving. Oppressed from the beginning of his tale by "a sense of insufferable gloom" and "an utter depression of the soul," the narrator speaks thereafter in dark and foreboding tones. He fancies that the house of Usher is surrounded by "pestilent and mystic vapor"; that in its walls "Perhaps the eye . . . might discover a barely perceptible fissure"; and that its furnishings breathe "an atmosphere of sorrow." He says it is difficult "to admit the identity" of Roderick Usher, yet he absorbs that identity quickly enough, chiding Usher for his "morbid acuteness of the senses" and "superstitious impressions" concerning the house. Since these were the narrator's initial sentiments, we may be amused to see them tossed to Usher, the so-called "hypochondriac." But the consequences of our narrator's psychosis, known as *projection,* are far too serious. When his instability becomes obvious, he claims to be "infected" by "the wild influences of [Usher's] . . . superstitions." For several nights after the lady Madeline's death, he and Roderick both suffer from nightmares, until finally he suggests, "I will read, and you shall listen: and so we will pass away this terrible night together." But only one of them will pass away, and it will not be the one who persistently takes an active role. His reading is interrupted by sounds he fears only he can hear; it is halted by the appearance of Madeline, whom—as far as we know—only he sees. Small wonder that Roderick finally calls him "MADMAN," or that he must sink all the evidence, characters and setting, in a "deep and dark tarn at my feet" (III, 273–97). Who can dispute his story? Those aware of its special pleading!

While many tales state Poe's reservations about Romantic ideas, others present them in his own versions. In "William Wilson," the narrator eventually learns that he is the source of his psychological troubles. Before that point, he is tormented by a strange person who bears the same name; competes with him in class and sports; never speaks above a whisper; copies his dress and manner; and in later years guards him against utter dissipation. Maddened by this "exquisite portraiture," Wilson forces the double into a duel, kills him, and hears—or perhaps even speaks—a final pronouncement:

> You have conquered, and I yield. Yet, hence-forward art thou also dead—dead to the World, to Heaven, and to Hope! In me didst thou exist—and, in my death, see by this image, which is thine own, how utterly thou hast murdered thyself. (III, 325)

The term *will,* meaning volition or selfish desire, appears throughout the tale. Wilson calls himself "self-willed," hates his double for "inter-ference with my will," but in the end submits to "his arbitrary will." (III, 300, 310, 323). Even his name repeats this pattern: Will-i-am Wil-son unscrambled reads "I am will, son [of] will." All of these factors indicate that the double is Wilson's diseased Self, or at least a mani-festation of that Self. Destroying the double is his ultimate act of selfish-ness, yet paradoxically, that deed effects his cure. Two voices unite to pronounce the old schism dead, thus climaxing a tale told by one man. Wilson has neither killed himself nor destroyed his conscience, for as the narrator he has obviously been alive and moral all along. In "William Wilson" Poe throws Romanticism a sliding curve: to know the Self, one must destroy all selfish desires—including the one for knowledge. The story thus anticipates *Eureka,* where he spells out the same conclusion more abstractly:

> . . . Attraction and Repulsion are Matter . . . [but] when . . . Matter
> . . . shall have returned into absolute Unity—it will then (to speak para-
> doxically for the moment) be . . . Matter no more . . . In sinking into
> Unity, it will sink into that Nothingness which . . . Unity must be
> . . . to have been created by the Volition of God.
> . . . The processes we have here ventured to contemplate will be renewed
> forever . . . at every throb of the . . . Heart Divine.
> And now—this Heart Divine—what is it? *It is our own.* (XVI, 310–11)

Of all his tales, the ratiocinatives present Poe's theme of self-knowl-edge, or identity, most clearly. In the figure of M. Dupin, for example, he comments directly on the "unreliable" narrators by balancing "the creative and the resolvent" faculties on one set of scales. Dupin's au-thority derives from his disciplined perception: his senses aid his mind ("To observe attentively is to remember distinctly . . ." [IV, 148]), and his mind serves his spirit (". . . the truly imaginative are never other-wise than analytic" [IV, 150]). This inward control permits Dupin to exercise virtues that few of the other narrators possess.

Dupin restrains the creative side of his mind, knowing "By undue profundity we perplex and enfeeble thought . . ." (V, 166). He be-lieves that Truth is simple, not twisted and obscure; that it rests in the actual, not the imagined; that it comes quickly to the man who can change his mind. Rigid theses dominate the unreliable narrators; Dupin's only dogma is flexibility. Principles, he believes, encourage "vast individual error," by obscuring the fact that "truth arises from the seemingly irrelevant" (V, 39). He accepts all "deviations from the plane of the ordinary" (V, 168), even when the ordinary itself is a deviation. Most men would hide a letter for which the police are search-ing; only a clever man would resort to the "sagacious expedient of not

attempting to conceal it at all" (VI, 48). By avoiding conventional sub-
tleties, Dupin can reach simple yet ingenious conclusions: the murderer
of the Rue Morgue is not a human being; only one person killed Marie
Rogêt. To get these answers, he challenges every assumption and questions every source. While reading Poe's other tales, we might practice
some of Dupin's caution. A story may well be self-indulgent, "conclu-
sive of little beyond the zeal of its inditer" (V, 21).

Dupin also controls his resolvent, or analytical, side by eliminating
personal bias. He gives detailed explanations of his cases because he
knows—as the unreliable narrators do not—that cause and effect are
often complex. Poe designs those lengthy analyses to show that a reasonable man is also imaginative—perhaps most legitimately so. In the
act of ratiocination Dupin becomes a creative artist, seeking to visualize
what he has never directly experienced. The unreliable narrators also
go this route, but they only create monstrous images of themselves.
Free of their blindness, Dupin actualizes for Poe the Romantic ideal
of an orderly and ordained universe. In the unity of Dupin's solutions
lies the secret of true correspondence, uniting man and the world according to the law of *Eureka:*

> He must have a care . . . lest, in pursuing too needlessly the superficial
> symmetry of forms and motions, he leave out of sight the really essential
> symmetry of the principles which determine and control them. (XVI, 302)

Despite his quarrel with didacticism, despite the claim that he
appeals only to "unripe boys and unsound men," [15] we may well remember Poe for his profound concern with philosophical, psychological, and yes, even moral truths. Haunted all his life by the enigma
of human identity, he confronted an age in which many writers had
reduced this problem to one of cheerful self-affirmation. That he chose
to follow a darker, less obvious path, refusing to sacrifice the complex
integrity of his art and moral vision, is the major reason for his twentieth-century fame. Today we honor Poe for his struggle, largely because we confront an age that has lost its innocence and longs for a
new form of self-esteem. Slowly and painfully we are learning that man
—especially the American—will endure only if he balances his warring
impulses, to rule and to serve, with the needs of his natural and social
environments. Halfway between freedom and bondage the Self and its
community meet; because Poe's tales teach this lesson unobtrusively
we can be certain of their "perfect consistency" and "absolute Truth."

[15] Paul Elmer More, "A Note on Poe's Method" in *Shelburne Essays on American
Literature,* First Series (New York: G. P. Putnam's Sons, 1907). p. 70.

Editor's Note

The following essays reflect in their diversity the extent of Poe's impact upon twentieth-century literary criticism. Their authors, a distinguished group of American, British, and Canadian scholars, represent the major critical avenues—historical (Williams, Walker, Griffith), theoretical (Martin, Winters, Garrison), and technical (Stauffer, Gargano, Robinson)—that intersect repeatedly in practical explication (Levin, Mooney, O'Donnell, Hill, Lauber, Daniel). If the collection favors "objective" readings, that is because the New Criticism happens to coincide with Poe's own critical ideals, spelled out well over a century ago. I have supplied references to the standard "Virginia" edition (see footnote 2) for almost all quotations. Any material I have added is either bracketed or signed ED. I wish to thank the staffs of the Firestone Library, Princeton University, and the Huntington Library, San Marino, California for their assistance in procuring research materials. My thanks also go to Professor Maynard Mack, who patiently read versions of the manuscript and offered expert advice. I am most indebted to my wife Barbara, who helped at every stage of this book's preparation. We are both grateful to Edward Davidson and Floyd Stovall, our teachers and friends, who first encouraged us to read—and reread—Poe's tales.

PART ONE

View Points

Harry Levin: Notes from Underground

. . . Poe might have been justified in designating his tales as notes from underground. Actually, he used such designations as *Phantasy-Pieces* or *Prose Romances,* and he considered other stratagems for presenting more or less unified collections. Working under pressure, he could not afford to become a devotee of the single precise word; instead, he seems to grope for several approximate synonyms, so that his writing smells of the thesaurus. Though his material is extremely concrete, his vocabulary tends to be abstract, so that his reader finds himself in the position of being instructed how he ought to react. For example, the adjective *terrific* is not a stimulus but a preconditioned response. Typography lends its questionable aid, with an excess of capitals, italics, dashes, and exclamation points. There are too many superlatives and intensitives and ineffables. There are also too many gallicisms like *outré, recherché,* and *bizarre,* repeated so loosely that Poe's French translator, Baudelaire, generally replaces them with a more elegant turn of phrase.

However, Poe seems to have hit his own mark when he called his first collection *Tales of the Grotesque and Arabesque,* utilizing a pair of romantic catchwords which he had probably encountered in Scott's essay "On the Supernatural in Fictitious Composition." The etymology of *grotesque,* deriving as it does from *grotto,* makes it particularly appropriate for his purposes. It means an artistic creation which is entirely imaginary, which has—in Milton's phrase—"no type in nature." It was paired against its classic antithesis, *sublime,* in the influential formula of Victor Hugo. *Arabesque,* on the other hand, is elusive by definition. It derives from the Arabic—or, rather, the Mohammedan—injunction against reproducing natural forms; hence its primary meaning pertains to geometrical design; and Poe's usage is strict as well as characteristic, in "Philosophy of Furniture," when he insists that "all upholstery . . . should be rigidly arabesque" [XIV, 104]. The term

---

had been extended to literary criticism by Friedrich Schlegel, who invoked it to formulate the interplay of contradictions and ironies in *Don Quixote*. Its broadest signification is the free play of fancy, a positive assertion of what is negatively implied by *grotesque*. Thus *arabesque* might aptly describe the art of Roderick Usher, who paints ideas in the form of "pure abstractions"; but Poe employs the catchword, more loosely, to characterize his hero's inhuman expression. Since both *arabesque* and *grotesque* mean much the same thing, in the sense of capricious or fanciful, efforts to subdivide Poe's tales between them are harder to support than Coleridge's problematic distinction between imagination and fancy. Yet gradations become important as we turn from Poe's outward and upward caprices to his more habitual direction, earthward.

His method, as enunciated in a well-known letter, was to intensify such differences of degree: "the ludicrous heightened into the grotesque, the fearful colored into the horrible, the witty exaggerated into the burlesque, the singular wrought out into the strange and mystical." [1] The common denominator is Poe's extremism, which not infrequently sets up its tensions between the sublime and the ridiculous. A fierce sense of humor, defensive and offensive, not unconnected with the violence of his worldview and the intellectuality of his reaction against it, comes out most sharply in his wars with his fellow literati. Into his imaginative constructions, comedy enters by way of hysteria; his cultivation of strangeness in the proportion leads him now to beauty, again to caricature. As a child of theatrical parents, it was fitting that he should become a "literary *histrio*," and that his technique of narration should be enlivened by "dramatism." The role he plays is essentially that of a monologuist, addressing us in his own person so compellingly that we soon find ourselves enacting the Coleridgean role of the Wedding Guest. To be specific, he plays the hypnotist, continually bent upon effecting a transference of emotions or sensations. That is why the short story is peculiarly his medium, since its concentration helps him to cast a spell—or, in his own critical terms, to aim at unity of effect. "During the hour of perusal, the soul of the reader is under the writer's control" [XI, 108]. Small wonder, then, if Poe's style is comparable to the patter of a stage magician, adept at undermining our incredulity with a display of sham erudition, scientific pretensions, quotations from occult authorities, and misquotations from foreign languages.

[1] *Letters*, I, 57-8.

Stephen L. Mooney: Poe's Detachment

The error that many of [Poe's] readers and critics have made, time after time, is to attribute to him an autobiographical, quasi-Wordsworthian theory of composition—the very reverse of what he set forth in his critical pieces. It is largely because of this error that a consideration of the total meaning of his tales has been delayed. Except in certain poems and in private letters, Poe is rarely interested in expressing his own emotions, as such. The tales are noteworthy for their attitude of dramatic objectivity, a fact that should have discouraged autobiographical interpretation, although it has not done so. Poe is detached. Even in the letters he is capable sometimes of playing skillfully upon the emotions of his correspondents (for example, John Pendleton Kennedy and Maria Clemm), who are treated as an audience that will respond to studied effects; he is aware of needing to turn the most subtle lights upon himself to project the desired image. To note the fact is not to accuse him of being insincere. Rather, it is to acknowledge that he was an artist, first and last, and his sincerity had to consist in creating effects. Anything less would have been a betrayal of his philosophy of composition, which may very nearly be read as his philosophy of life.

Least of all is he interested in the spontaneous overflow of powerful emotions recollected in tranquillity. Overflow was exactly the thing that he denounced; it was the *controlled* flow, carefully foreseen and regulated by deliberate calculation, that excited his imagination. He was not out to exploit his own emotions. He was scarcely interested in them. He was out to exercise the power of the artist over the reader's attention, and thereby to master and to manipulate the reader's responses. The naïve reader always assumes that he is in control of the words before him. The experienced reader of Poe knows better. Poe is in control.

Concerning such matters, he has been remarkably frank. He made certain observations in *Marginalia,* after finishing *The Mysteries of Paris* of Eugène Sue, that recall the protests of Milton's offended critics, objecting to the conscious manipulation of emotion for literary effect, even when this is necessary in fulfilling the requirements of a literary genre; Milton's detachment in "Lycidas" has been held against him.

"Poe's Detachment" by Stephen L. Mooney. From "Poe's Gothic Wasteland," Sewanee Review *LXX (1962), pp. 278–81. Copyright © 1962 by The University of the South. Reprinted by permission of* Sewanee Review *and Stephen L. Mooney.*

Like Milton, Poe in addressing his Muse—who no doubt would have to be some incarnation of the Imp of the Perverse—would not be ashamed to recommend to the Muse that she "somewhat loudly sweep the string." The professional is not carried away by his own perform-ance. He carries his audience away. As Poe says,

> In effect, the writer is always saying to the reader, "Now—in a moment— you shall see what you shall see. I am about to produce upon you a re-markable impression. Prepare to have your imagination, or your pity, greatly excited." [XVI, 104]

This is the tone of the magician whose sleight-of-hand will astonish the crowd in a profusion, an extravagant flourish, of skill. Whether Poe in his tales is presenting a Grand Guignol performance of the utmost grotesquerie, or an idyllic tableau of Landor's cottage miraculously transposed into the forests of New York State, or a picture of dead souls struggling to come alive, there is always the possibility that he is standing urbanely to the side, so as to say in the tones of a perfect gentleman, "Entrez, mesdames, messieurs; everything you see around you is false."

"In perusing a . . . pathetic chapter in 'The Mysteries of Paris,' " Poe declares, "we say to ourselves, without shedding a tear—'Now here is something that will move every reader to tears.' " Here, in short, is a perfectly achieved effect. Poe warns interpreters, however, against "over-reading":

> The philosophic motives attributed to Sue are absurd in the extreme. His first, and in fact his sole object, is to make an exciting book and therefore a saleable book. The cant (implied or direct) about the amelioration of society, etc., is but a very usual trick among authors, whereby they hope to add such a tone of dignity or utilitarianism to their pages as shall gild the pill of their licentiousness. [XVI, 104–5]

Poe's art is the art of those literalists of the imagination who, in Mari-anne Moore's over-famous picture, are capable of conjuring up real toads in imaginary gardens; or, in Coomaraswamy's terms, of demon-strating to the audience the grotesque immorality of casting false pearls before real swine. All that Poe ever said of simplicity as a literary doc-trine, or of continuity and unity, or of appropriate brevity, was encom-passed within the doctrine of effect: the calculation of the artist to involve the reader in the life of the fiction, so that an experience of reality would be forged in the consciousness, fully and permanently. Poe never says with Whitman, "Who are you now, holding me by the hand?" He is not so attractively ingenuous nor so ardently in love with the physical body of posterity. Poe is a spiritual aggressor. He moves in upon consciousness like an invading army. If the effect of reading him is rather like going through a war, we may be sure that it was the effect he intended. The reader does not forget. He knows that Poe has been there, arranging patterns of seriocomic destruction with the utmost *sang-froid.*

Terence Martin: The Imagination at Play

. . . in setting his imagination at play, Poe perforce fooled a society that had indentured the imagination to its own vision of success and progress. Historically, Poe's society refused to live by the imagination, contending (to put the matter briefly) that he who lives by the imagination dies by the imagination. Thus, it collaborated in being fooled. For what it could not imagine was Poe. Only Poe could imagine Poe; he presented himself as a hero of the imagination in a society that had no place for such a hero. His ultimate joke on the world would have been to make it his own in and by means of the imagination.

According to Johan Huizinga in *Homo Ludens*,[1] play is a non-material activity with no moral function. It can be, as he says, sportive or serious; historically, it has involved such things as stipulated limits of time and place and an element of uncertainty regarding its outcome. Huizinga's emphasis is on the importance of play as a developing function within a culture. The nineteenth century, he concludes, left little room for play: as civilization became more complex, it tended to subordinate play to its own serious business.

What Huizinga says about play enlarges our context for considering Poe's work. Poe's fondness for such things as puzzles and cryptograms, for example, reveals in a strict and elementary sense the imagination at play. More generally, the conception of play as an activity with no moral function suggests an important way of understanding the absence of a moral dimension in Poe's work: the imagination at play would have other, a-moral concerns simply by reason of its playing. As we have seen, however, Poe's imagination was not at home in his culture; if it was to play (and thus be a-moral), it necessarily took a-social and even anti-social postures. "The Cask of Amontillado" and

---

"The Imagination at Play" by Terence Martin. From Kenyon Review XXVIII *(1966), pp. 195–8. Copyright © 1966 by Kenyon College. Reprinted by permission of* Kenyon Review *and Terence Martin.*

[1] *Homo Luden: A Study of the Play Element in Culture.* (Boston: Beacon Press, 1955).

"The Black Cat," among other tales, illustrate clearly the manner in which Poe would fashion his material.

Perhaps no aphorism has had such sanction in our society as "crime does not pay." Our popular cultural forms have perennially shaped their material to dramatize this lesson. Anything else would seem to be, at least officially and as a serious proposal, unthinkable. Yet in "The Cask of Amontillado," perhaps his most popular and frequently anthologized story, Poe rejects the whole idea. Fifty years have passed since Montresor, the narrator, killed Fortunato; he has not been caught; and his tale re-enacts the joy of perfect vengeance. Poe constructs "The Cask of Amontillado" so as to emphasize its element of play: Fortunato (Fortunate One, or, more colloquially, Lucky) goes to his death in a clown's outfit, complete with "conical cap and bells": Montresor produces a trowel from beneath his cloak to prove that he is of the masons. Death and horror in "The Cask" contribute only to the narrator's satisfaction. The result is a story equipped with an astonishing anti-moral: crime pays. We, as audience, listen with interest to the boast-as-confession being made. Once it is made, we laugh and take it as some kind of joke; it would be murder to take it any other way [VI, 167–75].

Poe also reverses the familiar (and comfortable) tactic of domesticating the unknown and the potentially terrible. The narrator of "The Black Cat" tells us that, although he does not solicit belief for his "wild, yet most homely narrative," his purpose is "to place before the world, plainly, succinctly, and without comment, a series of mere household events." This is our entry to a story in which the narrator cuts out a cat's eye with his knife, hangs the cat from a tree because he loves it, and finally buries an ax in his wife's skull and walls her up in a standing position (together with a new one-eyed cat) in the basement. Our "series of mere household events" ends with the discovery of the corpse, "greatly decayed and clotted with gore," standing erect, with the cat upon its head [V, 143–55].

In "The Cask of Amontillado" and "The Black Cat," Poe inverts the modes of presentation and resolution most accepted in American letters of the time. Bryant and Longfellow, in their most representative work, had wedded the literary imagination to didacticism and domesticity; Hawthorne, with characteristic diffidence, frequently announced the moral of the tale and placed great stress on the value of hearth and home as agents of the heart. But Poe, militantly anti-didactic and mischievously anti-domestic, celebrates an act of perfect revenge and distills horror from domesticity. In "Berenice," the narrator speaks of the "inversion" that took place in his mind: the realities of the world seemed to him visionary, "while the wild ideas of the land of dreams" made up his everyday existence [II, 16–126]. Poe repeatedly introduces us to variations played on the theme of an inverted sense of reality. The narrator of "The Business Man" passes over such "eccentric pursuits" as those of merchant, lawyer, and dry-goods dealer to try the more "ordinary" occupations of Mud-Dabbling, Cur-Spattering, and Cat-tail-growing [IV, 122–33]. Whether "comic" or "serious," Poe's inversions come from an imagination that had liberated itself from the dictates of social orthodoxy.

Yvor Winters: Edgar Allan Poe: A Crisis in the History of American Obscurantism

In his criticism of Hawthorne's *Tales,* Poe outlines his theory of the short story. He defends the tale, as preferable to the novel, on the same grounds as those on which he defends the short poem in preference to the long. He states the necessity of careful planning and of economy of means.

He says: ". . . having conceived with deliberate care, a certain unique or single *effect* to be wrought out, he [the skillful literary artist] then invents such incidents—he then combines such events as may best aid him in establishing this preconceived effect" [XI, 108]. Now the word *effect,* here as elsewhere in Poe, means impression, or mood; it is a word that connotes emotion purely and simply. So that we see the story-teller, like the poet, interested primarily in the creation of an emotion for its own sake, not in the understanding of an experience. It is significant in this connection that most of his heroes are mad or on the verge of madness; a datum which settles his action firmly in the realm of inexplicable feeling from the outset.

Morella begins thus: "With a feeling of deep yet most singular affection I regarded my friend *Morella.* Thrown by accident into her society many years ago, my soul, from our first meeting, burned with fires it had never before known; but the fires were not of Eros, and bitter and tormenting to my spirit was the gradual conviction that I could in no manner define their unusual meaning or regulate their vague intensity." And *Ligeia:* "I cannot, for my soul, remember how, when, or even precisely where, I first became acquainted with the Lady Ligeia. Long years have since elapsed, and my memory is feeble through much

"Edgar Allan Poe: A Crisis in the History of American Obscurantism" by Yvor Winters. From In Defense of Reason (New York: The Swallow Press & William Morrow and Company, 1947), pp. 253–6. Copyright © 1947 by Yvor Winters. Reprinted by permission of The Swallow Press and Mrs. Yvor Winters.

suffering." *The Assignation:* "Ill-fated and mysterious man!—bewildered in the brilliancy of thine own imagination, and fallen in the flames of thine own youth." *The Tell-Tale Heart:* "True!—nervous—very, very dreadfully nervous I had been and am! but why *will* you say that I am mad?" *Berenice:* ". . . it *is* wonderful what a stagnation there fell upon the springs of my life—wonderful how total an inversion took place in the character of my commonest thought." *Eleonora:* "I am come of a race noted for vigor of fancy and ardor of passion. Men have called me mad; but the question is not yet settled, whether madness is or is not the loftiest intelligence—whether much that is glorious—whether all that is profound—does not spring from disease of thought—from *moods* of mind exalted at the expense of the general intellect." Roderick Usher, in addition, is mad; *The Black Cat* is a study in madness; *The Masque of the Red Death* is a study in hallucinatory terror. They are all studies in hysteria; they are written for the sake of the hysteria.

In discussing Hawthorne, however, Poe suggests other possibilities: "We have said that the tale has a point of superiority even over the poem. In fact, while the rhythm of this latter is an essential aid in the development of the poem's highest idea—the idea of the Beautiful—the artificialities of this rhythm are an inseparable bar to the development of all points of thought or expression which have their basis in *Truth.* But Truth is often, and in very great degree, the aim of the tale. Some of the finest tales are tales of ratiocination. Thus the field of this species of composition, if not in so elevated a region on the mountain of the Mind, is a tableland of far vaster extent than the domain of the mere poem. Its products are never so rich, but infinitely more numerous, and infinitely more appreciable by the mass of mankind. The writers of the prose tale, in short, may bring to his theme a vast variety of modes of inflections of thought and expressions (the ratiocinative, for example, the sarcastic, or the humorous) which are not only antagonistic to the nature of the poem, but absolutely forbidden by one of its most peculiar and indispensable adjuncts; we allude, of course, to rhythm. It may be added here, par parenthèse, that the author who aims at the purely beautiful in a prose tale is laboring at a great disadvantage. For Beauty can be better treated in the poem. Not so with terror, or passion, or horror, or a multitude of other such points" [XI, 108].

Poe speaks in this passage, not only of the tale of effect, to which allusion has already been made, but of the tale of ratiocination, that is, of the detective story, such as *The Gold Bug* or *The Murders in the Rue Morgue.* It is noteworthy that this is the only example which he gives of the invasion of the field of fiction by Truth; in other words, his primary conception of intellectual activity in fiction appears to be in the contrivance of a puzzle. Between this childish view of intellectuality, on the one hand, and the unoriented emotionalism of the tale of effect on the other, we have that vast and solid region inhabited by the major literary figures of the world, the region in which human experience is understood in moral terms and emotion is the result of that understanding, or is seen in relationship to that understanding and so judged. This region appears to have been closed to Poe; if we except the highly schematized and crudely melodramatic allegory of *William Wilson,* we have no basis for believing that he ever discovered it.

Joseph M. Garrison, Jr.: The Tales as Poems

If [Yvor] Winters is right, then Poe should surely meet with the fate which purposelessness deserves. But if he is wrong, it is the function of criticism at the present time—to use Arnold's apt phrase—to discover artistic integrity in Poe's work and thereby provide at least one substantial basis for an evaluation of his standing as a major American writer. . . .

The fact that Poe described one of his own prose compositions as a poem is highly significant for the possibility of artistic integrity in his serious work. His plea at the end of the preface to *Eureka* is suggestively applicable to many of his tales and sketches, and it supports some very educated guesses. Vincent Buranelli has pointed out similarities in tone, mood and theme between the poems and the tales; and he has reminded the forgetful reader that Poe freely introduced poems into his prose creations, and apparently introduced them without feeling that their inclusion would damage the effects.[1] The habit suggests that Poe considered the two genres compatible. "The Conqueror Worm," "To One in Paradise" and "The Haunted Palace" are incorporated in "Ligeia," "The Assignation" and "The Fall of the House of Usher" to sustain and intensify effects which have already been impressively accomplished by the prose narratives. Edward H. Davidson supports these observations when he says that Poe was encouraged,

---

"The Tales as Poems" by Joseph M. Garrison, Jr. From "The Function of Terror in the Work of Edgar Allan Poe," American Quarterly *XVIII (1966), pp. 137, 139–40. Copyright © 1966 by the Trustees of the University of Pennsylvania. Reprinted by permission of* American Quarterly *and Joseph Garrison.*

[1] *Edgar Allan Poe* (New York, 1961), p. 87.

specifically in the Grotesques, "to leave behind the accepted naturalistic
world around him and to explore the indeterminate regions which
poetry had suggested." "These tales," Davidson adds, "are indeed
'poems,' and Poe always remained a poet even when he was contribut-
ing some of his most uninspired narratives to the periodicals . . . ." [2]
Poe's own comments on the craft of short fiction in the reviews and
notices of Hawthorne's tales would suggest, moreover, that genre classi-
fication, as far as his own writing was concerned, was very artificial and
arbitrary; in fact the only determinants he supports uniformly and sys-
tematically are the principles of originality, brevity, totality and single
effect. Many of the observations in his discussions of Hawthorne's fiction are even appropriated from the early essays on poetry, such as the
"Letter to B——" and "Drake-Halleck." His definition of the kind of
tale which can provide "the fairest field which can be afforded by the
wide domains of mere prose, *for the exercise of the highest genius*"
(XIII, 151; italics mine) differs from his conception of the poem only
in the intensity with which it can excite the soul. The objective of the
stimulus is in both cases the same, the transmission of pleasure; and
this is "the end of all fictitious composition" (XIII, 145).

The popular term *short story* is evidently much too inclusive to substitute for the word *tale* as Poe uses it. He clearly distinguishes Irving's
"graceful and impressive narratives" (XIII, 153–54), or John Neal's
"magazine stories" (XIII, 154), from "that class of composition [the
tale] which, next to such a poem as I have suggested, should *best fulfil
the demands and serve the purposes of ambitious genius,* should offer it
the most advantageous field of exertion, and afford it the fairest opportunity of display . . ." (XIII, 152; italics mine). Such a tale should
demonstrate "true or commendable originality, . . . a peculiarity
springing from ever-active vigor of fancy—better still if from ever-pres-
ent force of imagination, giving its own hue, its own character to everything it touches, and, especially, *self impelled to touch everything*"
(XIII, 143).

The emphasis on originality in his discussions of the tale provides
additional evidence for similarity between Poe's theories of the poem
and the tale. He awarded William Cullen Bryant the highest poetical
honors because he had executed original conceptions which were "of
the very loftiest order of true Poesy" (IX, 302). Moreover, originality is
one of the poetic prerequisites enumerated in *"Ballads and Other
Poems"* (XI, 73). And Poe's own practical commitment to this poetic
virtue is unequivocally recorded in "The Philosophy of Composition,"
where he says that in writing "The Raven" his "first object (as usual)

[2] *Poe: A Critical Study* (Cambridge, 1957), p. 154.

was originality" (XIV, 203). The arguments for brevity, totality and single effect in the 1842 review of *Twice-Told Tales* also suggest that his poetic theory provided the basic assumptions that conditioned his definition of the tale. His discussion of these criteria draws explicit parallels between the characteristics of the two genres. The argument for brevity is a case in point: "The ordinary novel is objectionable, from its length, for reasons [analogous to those which render length objectionable in the poem] already stated in substance. As it cannot be read at one sitting, it deprives itself, of course, of the immense force derivable from *totality*" (XI, 107). The fact that Poe used an extensive discussion of his poetic principles as the introduction to his reviews of Hawthorne's tales offers of course the most substantial evidence that he considered the "brief prose tale" in its highest order an appropriate vehicle for the poetic sentiment, perhaps second only to the synthesis of poetry and music in verse.

William Carlos Williams: Edgar Allan Poe

Poe was not "a fault of nature," "a find for French eyes," ripe but unaccountable, as through our woollyheadedness we've sought to designate him, but a genius intimately shaped by his locality and time. It is to save our faces that we've given him a crazy reputation, a writer from whose classic accuracies we have not known how else to escape.

The false emphasis was helped by his Parisian vogue and tonal influence on Baudelaire, but the French mind was deeper hit than that. Poe's work strikes by its scrupulous originality, *not* "originality" in the bastard sense, but in its legitimate sense of solidity which goes back to the ground, a conviction that he *can judge* within himself. These things the French were *ready* to perceive and quick to use to their advantage: a new point from which to readjust the trigonometric measurements of literary form.

It is the New World, or to leave that for the better term, it is a *new locality* that is in Poe assertive; it is America, the first great burst through to expression of a re-awakened genius of *place*. . . . The local causes shaping [his] genius were two in character: the necessity for a fresh beginning, backed by a native vigor of extraordinary proportions,—with the corollary, that all "colonial imitation" must be swept aside. This was the conscious force which rose in Poe as innu-

"*Edgar Allan Poe*" *by William Carlos Williams. From* In the American Grain (*New York: Albert & Charles Boni, 1925), pp. 216–31. Copyright © 1925 by James Laughlin. Reprinted by permission of New Directions Publishing Corporation.*

merable timeless insights resulting, by his genius, in firm statements on the character of form, profusely illustrated by his practices; and, *second* the immediate effect of the locality upon the first, upon his nascent impulses, upon his original thrusts; tormenting the depths into a surface of bizarre designs by which he's known and which are *not at all* the major point in question.

Yet BOTH influences were determined by the locality, which, in the usual fashion, finds its mind swayed by the results of its stupidity rather than by a self-interest bred of greater wisdom. As with all else in America, the value of Poe's genius TO OURSELVES must be *uncovered* from our droppings, or at least uncovered from the "protection" which it must have raised about itself to have survived in any form among us—where everything is quickly trampled.

Poe "saw the end"; unhappily he saw his own despair at the same time, yet he continued to attack, with amazing genius seeking to discover, and discovering, points of firmness by which to STAND and grasp, against the slipping way they had of holding on in his locality. Either the New World must be mine as I will have it, or it is a worthless bog. There can be no concession. His attack was *from the center out.* Either I exist or I do not exist and no amount of pap which I happen to be lapping can dull me to the loss. It was a doctrine, anti-American. Here everything was makeshift, everything was colossal, in profusion. The frightened hogs or scared birds feeding on the corn— It left, in 1840, the same mood as ever dominant among us. Take what you can get. What you lack, copy. It was a population puffed with braggadocio, whom Poe so beautifully summarizes in many of his prose tales. . . .

Lowell, Bryant, etc., concerned poetry with literature, Poe concerned it with the soul; hence their differing conceptions of the use of language. With Poe, words were not hung by usage with associations, the pleasing wraiths of former masteries, this is the sentimental trap-door to beginnings. With Poe words were figures; an old language truly, but one from which he carried over only the most elemental qualities to his new purpose; which was, to find a way to tell his soul. Sometimes he used words so playfully his sentences seem to fly away from sense, the destructive! with the conserving abandon, foreshadowed, of a Gertrude Stein. The particles of language must be clear as sand. (See *Diddling*.) [V, 210–13]

This was an impossible conception for the gluey imagination of his day. Constantly he labored to detach SOMETHING from the inchoate mass — That's it:

His concern, the apex of his immaculate attack, was to detach a "method" from the smear of common usage—it is the work of nine tenths of his criticism. He struck to lay low the *"niaiseries"* of form and content with which his world abounded. It was a machine-gun fire; even in the slaughter of banality he rises to a merciless distinction. (See *Rufus Dawes*.) [XI, 131] He sought by stress upon construction to hold the loose-strung mass off even at the cost of an icy coldness of appearance; it was the first need of his time, an escape from the formless mass he hated. It is the very sense of a beginning, as *it is the impulse which drove him to the character of all his tales;* to get from sentiment to form, a backstroke from the swarming "population."

He has a habit, borrowed perhaps from algebra, of balancing his sentences in the middle, or of reversing them in the later clauses, a sense of play, as with objects, or numerals which he *has* in the original, disassociated, that is, from other literary habit; separate words which he feels and turns about as if he fitted them to his design with *some* sense of their individual quality: "those who belong properly to books, and to whom books, perhaps, do not quite so properly belong."

The strong sense of a beginning in Poe is in *no one* else before him. What he says, being thoroughly local in origin, has some chance of being universal in application, a thing they never dared conceive. . . . The difficulty is in holding the mind down to the point of seeing the *beginning* difference between Poe and the rest. One cannot expect to see as wide a gap between him and the others as exists between the Greek and the Chinese. It is only in the conception of a *possibility* that he is most distinguished. His greatness is in that he turned his back and faced inland, to originality, with the identical gesture of a Boone.

And for *that* reason he is unrecognized. Americans have never recognized themselves. How can they? It is impossible until someone invents the ORIGINAL terms. As long as we are content to be called by somebody else's terms, we are incapable of being anything but our own dupes. . . . it is precisely here that lies Hawthorne's lack of importance to our literature when he is compared with Poe; what Hawthorne *loses* by his willing closeness to the life of his locality in its vague humors; his lifelike copying of the New England melancholy; his reposeful closeness to the town pump—Poe *gains* by abhorring; flying to the ends of the earth for "original" material—

By such a simple, logical twist does Poe succeed in being the more American, heeding more the local necessities, the harder structural imperatives—by standing off to SEE instead of forcing himself too close. Whereas Hawthorne, in his tales, by doing what everyone else in France, England, Germany was doing *for his own milieu,* is no more than copying their *method* with another setting; does not ORIGINATE; has not a *beginning* literature at heart that must establish its own rules, own framework,—Poe has realized by adopting a more elevated mien.

This feeling in Poe's tales, that is, the hidden, under, unapparent part, gives him the firmness of INSIGHT into the conditions upon which our literature must rest, always the same, a local one, surely, but not of sentiment or mood, as not of trees and Indians, but of original fibre, the normal toughness which fragility of mood presupposes, if it will be expressive of anything— It is the expression of Poe's clearness of insight into the true difficulty, and his soundness of judgment.

To understand what Poe is driving at in his tales, one should read first NOT the popular, perfect—*Gold–Bug, Murders in the Rue Morgue,* etc., which by their brilliancy detract from the observation of his deeper intent, but the less striking tales—in fact all, but especially those where his humor is less certain, his mood lighter, less tightly bound by the incident, where numerous illuminating *faults* are allowed to become expressive, *The Business Man, The Man That Was Used Up, Loss of Breath, BonBon, Diddling, The Angel of the Odd*—and others of his lesser Tales.

It should be noted how often certain things take place—how often there is death but not that only; it is the body broken apart, dismembered, as in *Loss of Breath*—[II, 151–67]

Then, as in *Hop–Frog, The System of Dr. Tarr and Professor Fether* and the *Murders in the Rue Morgue*—the recurrent image of the ape. Is it his disgust with his immediate associates and his own fears, which cause this frequent use of the figure to create the emotion of extreme terror?—"Your majesty cannot conceive of the *effect* produced, at a masquerade, by eight chained orang-outangs, imagined to be real ones by the most of the company; and rushing in with savage cries, among the crowd of delicately and gorgeously habited men and women. The contrast is inimitable." [VI, 223]

Note, in *Silence—a Fable:* "sorrow and weariness and disgust with mankind and a longing for solitude." [II, 222]

Many colloquial words could be detached from Poe's usage if it were worth while, to show how the language he practices varies from English, but such an exercise would be of little value—*hipped, crack,* etc.—it does not touch bottom.

The Tales continue the theories of the criticism, carrying out what they propose:

1. In choice of material, abstract. 2. In method, a logical construction that clips away, in great part, the "scenery" near at hand in order to let the real business of composition *show*. 3. A primitive awkwardness of diction, lack of polish, colloquialism that is, unexpectedly, especially in the dialogues, much in the vein of Mark Twain.

One feels that in the actual composition of his tales there must have been for him, as they embody it in fact, a fascination other than the

topical one. The impulse that made him write them, that made him
enjoy writing them—cannot have been the puerile one of amazement,
but a deeper, logical enjoyment, in keeping with his own seriousness:
it is that of PROVING even the most preposterous of his inventions
plausible—that BY HIS METHOD he makes them WORK. They go: they
prove him potent, they confirm his thought. And by the very extreme
of their play, by so much the more do they hold up the actuality of
that which he conceives. . . .

Of his method in the Tales, the significance and the secret is: au-
thentic particles, a thousand of which spring to the mind for quotation,
taken apart and reknit with a view to emphasize, enforce and make
evident, the *method*. Their quality of skill in observation, their heat,
local verity, being *overshadowed* only by the detached, the abstract, the
cold philosophy of their joining together; a method springing so
freshly from the local conditions which determine it, by their emphasis
of firm crudity and lack of coordinated structure, as to be worthy of
most painstaking study— The whole period, America 1840, could be
rebuilt, psychologically (phrenologically) from Poe's "method."

PART TWO

Interpretations

From Earth to Ether: Poe's Flight into Space

by Charles O'Donnell

Arthur Gordon Pym, has been dead these many years, having perished, we are told, in an accident shortly after his return from a journey to the south. The faint tappings we have heard of late do not come from within the box, but from without; modern critics are attempting to loosen the nails pounded in by decades of indifference. In view of America's history of literary revivals and resurrections, it would not be surprising to see the lid fly suddenly off, letting Pym, like Mr. Shuttleworthy, spring into a sitting position and proclaim himself the author of a great masterpiece of literature.

Nothing that dramatic is likely to happen. But it is true that after one hundred years of bewilderment at the betrayal of sensibility evidenced in the French admiration of *The Narrative of A. Gordon Pym* [III, 1–242], American critics and literary historians began to praise or condemn the book on a firmer basis than the memory of a childhood reading. In the last few years three critics have given the work the benefit of sensitive and mature judgment.[1] To these I feel the need to add some thoughts, partly because someone, in memory of Poe, should cherish the vision of the young artist, happy in his artist's duplicity, juggling parts, manipulating symbols with ingenuity and dexterity toward an end he was destined never to achieve; and partly, too, because I can now say, with all the assurance of hindsight, that as an artist he was doomed almost from the start, that the philosophical ending was in the artistic beginning. Poe's works are all variations on a single persistent theme that finds its expression in forms ranging from pure

"From Earth to Ether: Poe's Flight into Space" by *Charles O'Donnell. From PMLA LXXVII (1962), pp. 85, 87–91. Copyright © 1962 by The Modern Language Association of America. Reprinted by permission of The Modern Language Association and Charles O'Donnell.*

[1] Edward H. Davidson, *Poe: A Critical Study* (Cambridge, Mass., 1957); Harry Levin, *The Power of Blackness* (New York, 1958); Patrick F. Quinn, *The French Face of Edgar Poe* (Carbondale, Ill., 1957).

hokum to pure speculation. Somewhere between the extremes, in a few stories, Poe manages to strike a chord familiar to the modern reader's ear. . . .

In *Pym* we see the dramatization in metaphor and symbol of the core idea that Poe later[2] expressed as abstract principle. The unfolding dread of annihilation and the unfolding search for unity not only control the method of the novel, they explain its failure.

It would be well to start by being sympathetic, by determining what Poe was trying to do. *Pym* is an ingenious book.

Let us assume, as a working hypothesis, that Poe meant the South Pole, "the region to the south," to suggest the perfect unity, the full design, the inner life. White, the "omni-color" as Poe calls it elsewhere, is the perfect blend of all colors, and broken up it becomes the separate colors, just as God broke up the unity of unparticled matter into the disunity of particled matter, which then struggles again toward reunification with the full design. The separate colors, the disparate elements, struggle to achieve the perfect condition of white, to blend into unity. Whiteness or light is therefore associated in the novel with death, with the giving up of the struggle, with submitting to the metamorphosis, the terrifying change to a bodiless condition of unity with the larger design. Black, on the other hand, is the absence of all color. Hence black cannot struggle to achieve perfection—it exists and can develop into nothing else, nor can it be broken up into separate parts. Black can only struggle to stay the same. Blackness or darkness is therefore associated with the desire to live in man's present condition on earth; it is the life wish—but a wish for "the primitive life of Earth" rather than "the ultimate life of Heaven."

Thus the novel starts appropriately with Pym in the dark, in the womb-like blackness of the ship's hold, ready to start his nine-month journey (from June 17 to March 22) to "continual daylight" near the South Pole. His ultimate symbolic birth into knowledge of the eternal is preceded by many symbolic deaths and rebirths. In the dark of the hold, when he sees the white fangs of some unknown beast gleaming through the gloom, he says, "I felt that my powers of body and mind were fast leaving me—in a word, that I was perishing, and perishing of sheer fright. My brain swam—I grew deadly sick—my vision failed—even the glaring eyeballs above me grew dim" [III, 29]. His mind and senses, his connection with the normal world, leave him as he approaches the annihilation of self suggested by whiteness. Pym is as frightened by the white teeth of the dog as the savages must have been

---

[2] The "later" work is *Eureka: a Prose Poem* (1848); XVI, 179–315.—ED.

by Peters' white teeth, which "were exceedingly long and protruding, and never even partially covered . . . by the lips" [III, 52]. When Nu-Nu is asked the motivation for the ambush, he points to his own black teeth. The savages were afraid of white teeth for the same reason Pym was—they meant death, the end of this life, of mental and bodily power. But Poe delights in reversal, especially where the senses are concerned—Pym discovers that the teeth are really the friendly teeth of his dog (who later springs at his throat). Pym says, "I experienced a sudden rush of blood to my temples—a giddy and overpowering sense of deliverence and reanimation" [III, 29]. This is a birth back into the world of struggle; his ultimate "deliverence" (Poe would have us believe) is at the end of the book.

Pym's reanimation is accomplished by a sudden rush of blood, of which substance there is certainly no shortage in the novel. Always it is suggestive of life, mystery, suffering, terror—in general, of the human situation. When Pym sees the word "blood" written, he says, "how chillily and heavily (disjointed, as it thus was, from any foregoing words to qualify or render it distinct) did its vague syllables fall, amid the deep gloom of my prison, into the innermost recesses of my soul!" [III, 41] (At least part of the reason for the terror in the word is its disjointedness from other words which would make it understandable. This is why life itself is terrifying in this novel. Things are only understood in the context of the larger design, which man cannot know.) The word "blood" (written in blood) on the piece of white paper seen dimly in the black hold is again as terrifying to Pym as is the combination of red and white to the savages when they see the white bear with the red claws and teeth. The spilling of human blood, like the omni-color white, means death to them.

White, black, and blood combine again in the ghost ship section to supply that particular combination of illusion and terror so often repeated throughout the work. The characters think they see a live, dark-skinned man on the ship, a black ship which gives them new hope of life. The man seems to smile constantly, and displays "a set of the most brilliantly white teeth." His red cap falls into the water, although the man does not seem to notice, "continuing his odd smiles and gesticulations." His companions are bloodless, "paler than marble." The white teeth appear to indicate a friendly smile. Inversion again. The man is dead and smiling the smile of death. White once again becomes meaningfully related to giving up the struggle for earthly life. The appearance of the black ship and the dark-skinned man had given them new hope in the struggle for existence, but in the middle of the illusion the discovery of the meaning of the white teeth "laid entirely prostrate every active faculty of mind and body." (Pym's dog, the white figure at

the South Pole, the white handkerchief, the white bear with red claws
and teeth, the white bird with blood on its talons—all paralyze the
faculties.) The shattered illusion of the ship destroys their "gay visions
of deliverance and joy." Not until the darkness of night are they re-
called to their senses [III, 110–15].

In most respects Pym and his friends are exactly the same, both in
motives and methods, as the savages, who, in a perfectly reasonable (as
far as they know) attempt to save themselves from the white menace,
kill a few people neatly and cleanly; and for this Pym calls them "the
most barbarous, subtle, and blood-thirsty wretches that ever contami-
nated the face of the globe" [III, 200]—this in the face of the drinking
of Parker's blood and the bloody massacre on board the *Grampus*. Pym
himself kills a few people in his successful masquerade escape from the
mutineers. He makes himself up as a corpse and sees the men on the
ship (like the natives, like Pym, like everyone in the novel) frightened
to death (literally in the case of the mate) by the appearance of red on
white, the blood on the chalky face. All the characters, black and white
alike, simply wish to preserve their lives; they are human beings.

But in one respect Pym differs from the savages whose principle of
civilization is based on the struggle to survive in the primitive state of
earthly life. Just as Poe embodies organic and inorganic in black and
white, so is there in Pym's ambivalent feeling toward life and death a
suggestion of the later repulsion-attraction idea. As Pym descends a
cliff (toward the end of his journey south) he finds his "imagination
growing terribly excited by thoughts of the vast depth yet to be descended, and the precarious nature of the pegs and soap-stone holes
which were [his] only support." It is in vain that he attempts to rid
himself of this excitement. The more he struggles not to think, "the
more intensely vivid" become his conceptions. The fancies begin "creating their own realities," and he becomes "consumed with the irrepressible desire of looking below." His whole soul is "pervaded with *A
Longing to Fall*." Then, with a "phantom voice" screaming in his ears,
he sinks down and plunges into the arms of a figure standing below.
(The scream in *Pym* seems to accompany the possibility of death, and
it is the presence of the scream at the end of the novel which helps us
to realize the symbolic significance of the pole.) The idea of "ultimate
escape" passes "like a shadow" through his mind [III, 229–30]. Again
shadows are connected with the idea of preserving this life. But as soon
as that shadow passes, Pym has an uncontrollable desire to fall. He
desires to die. It is this death urge—or higher life urge—which motivates the search for the pole, or for the Auroras which the characters
are not even sure exist. During this search thus motivated by an unconscious longing for unity, the sufferings and delusions of the organic

life continue; the struggle must go on, even though the end, the ultimate destiny, is inevitable.

Thus Pym is born into death, he achieves symbolic knowledge of the inorganic life, when he sees rising before him the shrouded human figure with skin "the perfect whiteness of the snow" [III, 242]. The dark struggle for survival is replaced by a numbness (blood, the life force, ceasing to circulate) of mind and body, a dreaminess of sensation. He returns, of course, but never to define his mystical insight. The unknown cannot be told. Even Pym did not seem to gain any ultimate knowledge. A mystical or symbolic apprehension of the universal design will not end the primitive life on earth. The journey does not end until death; after the vision, Pym simply returns, in the famous unexplained way, to his corporeal life. . . .

The tension between body and soul, unity and individuality, attraction and repulsion, the universe and the world, manifests itself in a ticklish problem: commitment to the ordinary world of men demands that the story have a sense of completeness, that Poe explain how Pym escapes and returns; commitment to the universe demands that the story end with the vision of whiteness. Poe, in a choice foreshadowing his future, decided in favor of the universe, even at the expense of the truncated ending.

This is not to say that Poe was ignoring the demands of the world. Pym did get back safely, that we are told; the question is therefore how. Since Poe's purpose—to climax with Pym's vision of universal whiteness—precluded his giving the details of the return, he tried instead to reveal the facts through indirection by experimenting with form, by suggesting the end of the story in episodes at the beginning and center. That his effort wasn't a crashing success is testified to by the number of readers it has eluded.

I grant that it isn't obvious. I think Poe meant to give a clue to his intention in the way he ordered the book, dividing it roughly in half, making all events lead up to and away from Pym's rescue by the *Jane Guy* at the end of the central chapter, each event in the first half paralleling an event in the second half. At the beginning, the characters set sail in a small boat; there is a wreck from which they are rescued; Pym is confined in the hold; there is treachery in the form of a mutiny; they escape by killing treacherous men; and they sail in a disabled ship toward the equator and are rescued. In the second half they sail away from the equator toward an island; there is treachery; they are confined in the hills; they escape by killing treacherous men; they set sail in a small boat toward the pole; and—I assume Poe wants me to see—there is a wreck from which they are rescued, thus allowing Pym to get home.

The general impression of parallel events is reinforced by other similar details in the two halves (some of them seemingly without other purpose than to call our attention to the order in the book): On July 5 (summer north of the equator) a man falls overboard from the *Grampus;* on January 10 (summer south of the equator) a man falls overboard from the *Jane Guy.* On the *Grampus,* Pym looks into a mirror and almost swoons—so with Too-wit on the *Jane Guy.*

I dare say that Poe wanted his readers to understand that Pym was rescued by a ship: a technical explanation of certain weather conditions that would make reasonable Pym's escape from death at the end of the book is given in a long passage at the beginning of Chapter xiv, just after Pym and Peters are picked up by the *Jane Guy:*

> On the sixteenth of September, being in the vicinity of the Cape of Good Hope, the schooner encountered her first gale of any violence since leaving Liverpool. In this neighborhood, but more frequently to the south and east of the promontory (we were to the westward), navigators have often to contend with storms from the northward, which rage with great fury. They always bring with them a heavy sea, and one of their most dangerous features is the instantaneous chopping round of the wind, an occurrence almost certain to take place during the greatest force of the gale. A perfect hurricane will be blowing at one moment from the northward or northeast, and in the next not a breath of wind will be felt in that direction, while from the southwest it will come out all at once with a violence almost inconceivable. A bright spot to the southward is the sure forerunner of the change, and vessels are thus enabled to take the proper precautions. (III, 150–51)

This description helps to explain how Pym and Peters are saved at the Pole. Their boat is rushing southward "with a hideous velocity." Ahead of them "a luminous glare" arises; it is consistent with Pym's explanation of the erratic storms to believe that the brightness is the forerunner of a change in the wind, so that from the south now would come "rushing and mighty, but soundless winds, tearing up the enkindled ocean in their course." Pym has already felt a "numbness of body and mind—a dreaminess of sensation." With his senses thus dimmed (even when his perceptions are normal they are not to be trusted) Pym sees what he takes to be the white and shrouded figure, "very far larger in its proportions than any dweller among men" [III, 241–42]. I am convinced that Poe is once again rescuing Pym, that Pym actually sees something: a figurehead, sail, or prow of a ship being blown toward him by the new winds from the south.

To reveal the details of the rescue, Poe used the device of the miniature episode. At the beginning of the novel, Augustus (instead of Peters) is with Pym in a small boat. The wind "blew freshly from the south-west." Augustus' eyes are glazed, and like Nu-Nu, he falls to the bottom of the boat. Pym himself is for a time "paralyzed . . . beyond the possibility of making any exertion," and we remember that at the end he does not pick a floating animal out of the water because there came over him a sudden listlessness. Pym is incapable of managing the *Ariel.* Because the boat is "going through the water at a terrible rate," Pym is convinced that "a fierce wind and strong ebb tide were hurrying [them] to destruction." When the ship hits the *Ariel* (after a scream like the scream of the birds at the end) Pym falls unconscious on top of his companion, and when he wakes up, he is in the cabin of the *Penguin* [III, 7–11]. The same reaction at the end would explain why, on a literal level, the book concludes where it does: Pym and Peters are unconscious, thrown into the whirling water (just like Augustus at the beginning who woke to find himself "beneath the surface, whirling round and round with inconceivable rapidity"). Thus we read (substituting the name Peters for Augustus): "Yet, as the reader has seen, both Augustus and myself were rescued; and our deliverance seemed to have been brought about by two of those almost inconceivable pieces of good fortune which are attributed by the wise and pious to the special interference of Providence" [III, 12].

There is another rescue at the center of the book, again with many parallels to the end. Three men are in a boat they cannot control; Augustus, like Nu-Nu at the end, lies insensible with his arm black. The sea is warm from an oppressively hot sun, and when the ship rolls over, "the sea in all directions" is "much agitated and full of strong whirlpools." The men are rescued, but not before they are reduced to childish, irrational beings. Pym says, in a statement that might also apply to the ending of the book, "both Peters and myself recovered entirely from the effects of our late privation and dreadful suffering, and we began to remember what had passed rather as a frightful dream from which we had been happily awakened, than as events which had taken place in sober and naked reality" [III, 139–50].

The frightful dream and the sober reality—the quotation hints at the problem Poe faced in *Pym.* Wanting to have his artistic cake and eat it too, Poe builds toward the grand vision of eternity at the same time that he plants in his text obscure bits of evidence to show that Pym and Peters are again being deluded, that really there is a rational explanation for the seemingly miraculous vision that would conform to the strictest demands of "sober and naked reality." The prosaic resolution works against the theme of ultimate life through physical death.

Poe preferred the vision. He continued to experiment in art forms, but he never discovered the key to shaping the world in a way that would enable human beings "to depart, yet live—to leave the world,

yet continue to exist" [II, 61].[3] The infolding embrace of self and the
unfolding search for universal being define the terms of man's existence on earth; but the marriage of opposites, the grand resolution,
comes only when Poe flies from the life of man and apotheosizes the
abstract "Life—Life—Life within Life." . . .

Poe's flight to the abstract is not so important to his readers as the
stories he wrote along the way. It is between the unsuccessful experiment of *Pym* and the final commitment to pure intellect that Poe discovered his true subject for fiction. It is in his torturous descriptions of
the split between man and the objective world that Poe strikes us as
most modern. The best of his short stories deal with the impact on
man's inner reality of an upsetting of the normal balance between attraction and repulsion.

From the concrete to the abstract, from man to God, the pattern is
the same: life is action and reaction. For God, life is the rhythm of self-
diffusion and self-concentration; life is the expansion of pleasure into
an infinity of imperfect pleasures, and the joy of existence felt at con-
traction. For the universe, life is the push of repulsion and the pull of
attraction. For the angel, life is the contrast between the suffering of
the organic and the pleasure of the inorganic. And for man, life is the
conflict between the demands of the soul and the demands of the body,
between the fear of annihilation and the longing for unification.

The large majority of men do not feel the conflict, do not live with
any intensity. They are not conscious of the absurd tug of war between
human soul and flesh. A fair share of Poe's stories satirize the men of
this sane world of affairs whose thought and feeling are limited to the
burrowing pursuit of their own petty goals. Poe at his best probes into
the condition of the mind in men who feel life most sharply because it is
in jeopardy, men for whom the ordinary world ceases to have meaning
and value.

[3] The quotation is from "The Unparalleled Adventure of One Hans Pfall" (June,
1835).—ED.

The "Legitimate" Sources of Terror in "The Fall of the House of Usher"

by I. M. Walker

Poe did not allow . . . criticisms of his work in general and "The Fall of the House of Usher" in particular to pass unanswered, and in his "Preface" to *Tales of the Grotesque and Arabesque* (1840) he replied to the false notion ". . . which has induced one or two critics to tax me, in all friendliness, with what they have been pleased to term 'Germanism' and gloom." . . . he went on to state in forthright and unambiguous terms that the terror he wrote about was not fantastic or "German," but was realistic and based upon true principles of human nature and conduct:

> If in many of my productions terror has been the thesis, I maintain that terror is not of Germany, but of the soul—that I have deduced this terror only from its legitimate sources, and urged it only to its legitimate results. [I, 151]

Poe's defence of his work in this "Preface" has too often been underestimated by his critics, and this is nowhere more apparent than in the considerable body of critical commentary on "The Fall of the House of Usher." It has been generally recognized that the tale concerns the disintegration of Roderick Usher, but the "legitimate sources" of terror about which Poe stated he was writing have been largely neglected. This paper will seek to provide a rational interpretation of two important and at first sight characteristically "German" elements in "The Fall of the House of Usher": the sinister black tarn which dominates the environment, and Madeline Usher's return from the tomb to destroy her brother. This investigation of the "legitimate sources" of terror in the tale leads not only to an understanding of Roderick Usher's strange appearance and conduct, and Madeline's seemingly supernat-

"The 'Legitimate' Sources of Terror in 'The Fall of the House of Usher' " by I. M. Walker. From Modern Language Review LXI (*1966*), *pp. 585–92. Copyright* © *1966 by The Modern Humanities Research Association. Reprinted by permission of* Modern Language Review *and I. M. Walker.*

ural resurrection, but also to a revaluation of the narrator's position in
the tale.

The opening scene contains the ingredients of a conventional Gothic
melodrama: the solitary rider, passing through "a singularly dreary
tract of country," is oppressed by "a sense of insufferable gloom," when,
as evening draws on, he approaches the lonely, dilapidated, and melancholy House of Usher. The climax of the scene occurs when the rider
reins his horse at the brink of "a black and lurid tarn that lay in un-
ruffled lustre by the dwelling," and experiences "a shudder more thrill-
ing than before" as he sees in the silent black waters "inverted images
of the grey sedge, and the ghastly tree-stems, and the vacant and eye-
like windows" [III, 273–74]. Although the gloom of this scene undoubt-
edly prepares the reader for the melancholy happenings at the House
of Usher, the black tarn is not simply part of an elaborate Gothic
décor. . . . "The Fall of the House of Usher" concerns the total disintegration of Roderick Usher, and in accord with Poe's theory of the
unity of a work of art, the sinister tarn which so appals the narrator in
the first scene, contributes actively to Usher's destruction.

The black tarn is associated with imagery of desolation (grey sedge)
and decay (rotting trees), as well as with the house itself, which, as the
poem "The Haunted Palace" makes quite clear, operates throughout
as a symbol of Roderick Usher. An emblematic statement of the relationship between the house-man symbol and the tarn is made when the
narrator sees them joined together by a crack in the structure of the
mansion, the crack representing the imminent collapse of Roderick
Usher's ruined personality:

> Perhaps the eye of a scrutinising observer might have discovered a barely
> perceptible fissure, which, extending from the roof of the building in
> front, made its way down the wall in a zigzag direction, until it became
> lost in the sullen waters of the tarn. [III, 277]

The relationship between Roderick Usher and his physical surroundings, and the influence which these surroundings of the decayed house
and the stagnant tarn have exerted on his life and the lives of his an-
cestors, is recognized and meditated upon by the narrator early in the
tale:

> . . . while running over in thought the perfect keeping of the character
> of the premises with the accredited character of the people, and while
> speculating upon the possible influence which the one, in the long lapse
> of centuries, might have exercised upon the other. [III, 275]

The narrator also observes what he calls an "atmosphere" around the
house and tarn, which he rightly believes to have noxious qualities:

. . . about the whole mansion and domain there hung an atmosphere peculiar to themselves and their immediate vicinity—an atmosphere which had no affinity with the air of heaven, but which had reeked up from the decayed trees, and the grey wall, and the silent tarn—a pestilent and mystic vapour, and leaden-hued. [III, 276]

Poe is using the word "atmosphere" in this passage in a special physical sense that is rarely used to-day, and which the *New English Dictionary* defines as 'a gaseous envelope surrounding any substance', and quite distinct from the air. The narrator is careful to point out that the "atmosphere" he sees surrounding the house and tarn "had no affinity with the air of heaven." The popular *Cyclopaedia* compiled by Abraham Rees supplies a nineteenth-century usage of the word that is close to Poe's: "ATMOSPHERE of solid or consistent Bodies, is a kind of sphere formed by the effluvia, or minute corpuscles emitted from them." [1]

It is not only the narrator, however, who can recognize the influence which this pestilential "atmosphere" has on Roderick Usher, for Usher himself is in the agonizing position of being able to follow the progress of his own disintegration, while being powerless to prevent it. He tells the narrator of the deleterious effect which his physical environment has had on his life:

—an effect which the *physique* of the grey walls and turrets, and of the dim tarn into which they all looked down, had, at length, brought about upon the *morale* of his existence. [III, 281]

Roderick Usher has a firm belief in the sentience of inorganic matter, and significantly he sees the reason for this belief in the "atmosphere" arising from the stagnant tarn and decayed house. Moreover, he states clearly that the "atmosphere" has been responsible not only for the strange characteristics of his family, but for his own pitiful condition also:

Its evidence—the evidence of the sentience—was to be seen, he said (and here I started as he spoke); in the gradual yet certain condensation of an atmosphere of their own about the waters and the walls. The result was discoverable, he added, in that silent, yet importunate and terrible influence which for centuries had moulded the destinies of his family, and which made *him* what I now saw him—what he was. [III, 286–87]

On the night of the catastrophe the noxious "atmosphere" is particularly dense, and gathers around the house like a shroud:

[1] Abraham Rees, *The Cyclopaedia or Universal Dictionary of Arts, Sciences and Literature* (1819), vol. III, n.p.

But the under surfaces of the huge masses of agitated vapour, as well as
all terrestrial objects immediately surrounding us, were glowing in the
unnatural light of a faintly luminous and distinctly visible gaseous exhala-
tion which hung about and enshrouded the mansion. [III, 291]

The narrator realizing the dangers of this "atmosphere" warns Usher
away from the open window, telling him ". . . 'the air is chilling and
dangerous to your frame,' " and rightly suggesting that the foul airs
" '. . . have their ghastly origin in the rank miasma of the tarn.' " [III,
292]

It was accepted as a scientific fact at the time that odours and gases
arising out of foul water or decayed matter were the causes of physical
and mental illnesses. Thomas C. Upham, for example, the highly es-
teemed American philosopher and psychologist, wrote in his *Elements
of Mental Philosophy*:

> There is another gas, the FEBRILE MIASMA, which is found, on being
> inhaled, to affect the mind also, by first affecting the sanguineous fluid.
> But this gas diminishes instead of increasing the volume of blood; as is
> indicated by a small contracted pulse, and an increasing constriction of
> the capillaries. As in the case of the nitrous oxide gas, the mental exercises
> are rendered intense and vivid by the febrile miasma; but the emotions
> which are experienced, instead of being pleasant, are gloomy and painful.
> The trains of thought, which are at such times suggested, and the cre-
> ations of the imagination are all of an analogous character, strange, spec-
> tral and terrifying.[2]

. . . There is a close resemblance between what Thomas Upham and
other authorities said about the effects of miasma on the human mind
and constitution, and Roderick Usher's deranged mental and physical
condition. The letter which the narrator receives calling him to the
House of Usher betrays Roderick's derangement: "The MS. gave evidence of nervous agitation. The writer spoke of acute bodily illness—of
a mental disorder which oppressed him" [III, 274]. Thomas Upham
pointed out that "febrile miasma" produced a diminished blood supply
and a slow pulse in those exposed to its vapours, and the results of such
an exposure can be observed in Usher's physical appearance. The narrator speaks of the "wan being" before him, and is horrified by his
"cadaverousness of complexion," and the "ghastly pallor of the skin."

Throughout the tale Usher is in an acute state of terror arising from
undefined causes:

> To an anomalous species of terror I found him a bounden slave. "I shall
> perish," said he, "I *must* perish in this deplorable folly. . . . In this un-

[2] Thomas C. Upham, *Elements of Mental Philosophy*, two vols. (Portland, 1837), I,
409–10.

nerved—in this pitiable condition—I feel that the period will sooner or later arrive when I must abandon life and reason together, in some struggle with the grim phantasm FEAR." [III, 280]

This state of terror can also be traced back to the stagnant tarn and its miasmic "atmosphere." Mental philosophers including Thomas Upham postulated that effluvia arising from decayed matter could produce serious mental and emotional disturbances in those exposed to them. John MacCulloch, the eminent Scottish doctor, in a standard and authoritative work on miasma, describes an irrational state of terror produced by miasmata, which is remarkably similar to Usher's condition:

> Despair and fear, analogous passions, are, rather than anger and its modes, the two great mental affections of hypochondriasis; and hence it is that fear chiefly, often attends the paroxysm of this obscure remittent. This however is true of marsh fevers generally, whether remittent or intermittent, and under all the modes of these diseases. So remarkable indeed is this mental condition, fear, in the disorders of this nature, that in some parts of the Mediterranean where these fevers are endemic, the only name by which they are known to the common people, is Scanto; fear or fright.

MacCulloch also observed that miasma could produce an adverse effect upon the "intellectual faculties":

> The conditions of the intellect then which I would here remark, are those of torpidity on the one hand and excitement on the other; the first consisting in an inability to think, sometimes attended by confusion of thought, and the other in an excessive flow or crowding of ideas, necessarily, in many cases, attended also with similar confusion.[3]

The narrator recognizes in Usher precisely similar states of alternating excitement and depression, as well as the confusion of thought mentioned by MacCulloch: "In the manner of my friend I was at once struck by an incoherence—an inconsistency: . . . His action was alternately vivacious and sullen" [III, 279].

Thomas Upham, in the passage previously quoted from *Elements of Mental Philosophy,* said that in those affected by the "febrile miasma," the "creations of the imagination" would be "strange, spectral and terrifying." The same adjectives could be used to describe exactly Roderick Usher's peculiar artistic compositions. His music is distorted by a "morbid condition of the auditory nerve," and he plays "a certain singular perversion and amplification of the wild air of the last waltz of Von Weber" [III, 283]. In his "fantastic" impromptu poem "The

---

[3] John MacCulloch, *An Essay on the Remittent and Intermittent Diseases,* two vols. (1828), 1, 61 and 70. MacCulloch's book was published in Philadelphia in 1830 by Carey and Lea.

Haunted Palace" Usher writes about the break-up of his own mind, while his "phantasmagoric" painting could be accurately described as "strange, spectral and terrifying":

> A small picture presented the interior of an immensely long and rectangular vault or tunnel, with low walls, smooth, white and without interruption or device. . . . No outlet was observed in any portion of its vast extent, and no torch, or other artificial source of light was discernible; yet a flood of intense rays rolled throughout, and bathed the whole in a ghastly and inappropriate splendour. [III, 283]

The poem, the music, and the painting are all compulsive revelations of Usher's emotional and intellectual derangement.

Following the entombment of Madeline, Roderick's disintegration accelerates. His physical appearance is more spectral and startling than ever: "The pallor of his countenance had assumed, if possible, a more ghastly hue" and his mental derangement has obviously become extreme. Moods of "mad hilarity" alternate with periods of silent vacancy, and terror has taken complete possession of his mind: "The once occasional huskiness of his tone was heard no more; and a tremulous quaver, as if of extreme terror, habitually characterized his utterance" [III, 289].

But what is perhaps more surprising is what happens to the narrator after Madeline's entombment. His seemingly detached and rational earlier attitudes for the most part disappear, and his mind begins to submit to the power of Roderick's mad fantasies: "I felt creeping upon me, by slow yet certain degrees, the wild influences of his own fantastic yet impressive superstitions" [III, 290]. What happens to the narrator after Madeline's death is not altogether unprepared for earlier in the tale, for despite his façade of rationalism, he has shown signs of an imaginative and highly impressionable mind. His first sight of the House of Usher had affected him with a sense of gloomy foreboding quite beyond rational explanation: "I know not how it was—but, with the first glimpse of the building, a sense of insufferable gloom pervaded my spirit" [III, 273]. Similarly his feelings when he first sees Madeline Usher are impressionistic and irrational:

> While he spoke, the lady Madeline (for so was she called) passed slowly through a remote portion of the apartment, and, without having noticed my presence, disappeared. I regarded her with an utter astonishment not unmingled with dread—and yet I found it impossible to account for such feelings. [III, 281]

On the night of the catastrophe the narrator experiences the same depression and terror which had oppressed Roderick throughout the tale, and it becomes obvious that his mental balance is being disturbed by his environment, and by Roderick's madness. He cannot sleep, and tries in vain to "reason off" the depression which has taken hold of him: "But my efforts were fruitless. An irrepressible tremour gradually pervaded my frame; and, at length, there sat upon my very heart an incubus of utterly causeless alarm." Even before Roderick comes to his room the narrator is in a state of extreme terror, which is an extension of Roderick's own condition:

> Overpowered by an intense sentiment of horror, unaccountable yet unendurable, I threw on my clothes with haste (for I felt I should sleep no more during the night), and endeavoured to arouse myself from the pitiable condition into which I had fallen, by pacing rapidly to and fro through the apartment. [III, 290]

Madeline's escape from the tomb seems at first to be real because the narrator believes it and tells about it in such a compelling and dramatic manner, but on close inspection doubts occur about the reality of the whole episode. Roderick claims to hear Madeline's feet on the stairs and outside the room, but it must be remembered that his senses are deranged, and he also makes the impossible claim to have heard her "first feeble movements" in the coffin many days before. Considered from a realistic viewpoint Madeline's resurrection is incredible, and what Roderick and the narrator believe they see is an illusion, which, in Thomas Upham's words, ". . . happens at the moment to be so distinct, as to control their belief and impose itself upon them for a reality." [4] We learn that before her death Madeline suffered a long and distressing illness that wasted her body, and this being so, she could hardly be in a condition to break out of her coffin eight days after being entombed. Moreover, her body is buried "at great depth" in a vault beneath the house, which had been lined with copper, to keep out damp from the tarn. This vault had at one time been used "for the worst purposes of a donjon-keep" [III, 288] and is equipped with a copper lined door of "massive iron." More recently it had been used as a powder store, and its copper lining, while evidently unsuccessful as damp-proofing (it is "small, damp . . ."), kept out both light and air. Further, Poe is careful to point out that the coffin lid is screwed down and the iron door bolted when the narrator and Roderick leave the vault. Even if Madeline does revive in her coffin it is impossible to believe that after eight days in the tomb she could emerge alive.

The reading of "The Mad Tryst" which prefigures Madeline's ap-

---

[4] *Elements of Mental Philosophy*, I, 415. Illusions were considered a common product of mental derangement by contemporary authorities on medicine and "mental philosophy." See, for example, Benjamin Rush, *Medical Inquiries and Observations Upon the Diseases of the Mind* (Philadelphia, 1812), chapter xv.

pearance is necessary both to sustain the tension of the tale, and to precipitate the catastrophe. When Roderick comes to his room mad through fear, the narrator reads "The Mad Tryst" in the naïve hope that ". . . the hypochondriac, might find relief (for the history of mental disorder is full of similar anomalies)" [III, 292]. But Roderick's madness is beyond the stage when such diversions can help, and ironically instead of distracting Roderick, the reading heightens his alarm and terror. For a brief period the narrator retains enough fragments of his reason to resist Roderick's hallucination, and realizes that the "cracking and ripping sound" which he hears while reading how the knight broke into the hermit's dwelling is due to the coincidence of an electrical storm outside: "It was, beyond doubt, the coincidence alone which arrested my attention" [III, 293]. To Usher's deranged mind, however, the supernatural happenings in "The Mad Tryst" and the sounds of the storm suggest only one meaning—that Madeline has risen from her tomb and is about to destroy him. In this fantasy the narrator eventually acquiesces, overwhelmed by the reality of Usher's terror, and completely unnerved by the sounds of the storm and his grotesque surroundings.

Madeline's return from the tomb has been accepted as a literal fact by Poe's critics, though most of them have avoided committing themselves on the problem of exactly how Madeline achieves her resurrection.[5] It is a tribute to Poe's skill as a writer that he has created through the narrator a situation which appears as real to most of his readers as it does to the narrator and Roderick Usher, but this does not mean that Poe intended Madeline's reappearance to have any reality outside the deranged minds of the two protagonists in the tale. In a letter to James Russell Lowell, Poe said that he considered "The Fall of the House of Usher" to be one of his finest productions,[6] and this being so, it is unlikely he would have compromised the principles he outlined in his "Preface" by using such a "German" contrivance as a physical resurrection eight days after death. The purpose of the tale is to explore mental derangement rather than to present an elaborate Gothic horror story, and the terror it contains is psychological not "German."

[5] It has recently been suggested that Madeline's resurrection is due to her being a vampire. See J. O. Bailey, "What Happens in 'The Fall of the House of Usher'?," *American Literature,* 35 (1964), 445–67; also Lyle H. Kendall, "The Vampire Motif in 'The Fall of the House of Usher'," *College English,* 34 (1963), 450–3. But this theory completely disregards the principles Poe described in his "Preface," which were directly inspired by criticism that "The Fall of the House of Usher" contained supernatural or "German" motifs.

[6] *Letters,* I, 258.

The Dual Hallucination
in "The Fall of the House of Usher"

by John S. Hill

At the end of Edgar Allan Poe's "The Fall of the House of Usher," Madeline Usher escapes from her tomb and throws herself upon her brother, Roderick, bearing him to his death.

The general reading of this scene accepts Madeline as alive.

Yet this interpretation is erroneous, for the facts in the tale prove that Madeline is dead and, consequently, that the Madeline who hurls herself upon Roderick can only be a hallucination. Moreover, Poe was too conscientious a craftsman to ignore facts written into a story; and Poe's craftsmanship is the clue which, if followed, proves that Madeline's final appearance is made as a ghost.

Madeline was afflicted by "a settled apathy, a gradual wasting away of the person, and frequent although transient affections of a partially cataleptical character . . ." [III, 282]. One evening, shortly after the narrator has arrived at the House of Usher, Roderick tells him that Madeline is dead and that he will preserve her corpse for a fortnight in a vault in the building rather than bury her in the remote family burial ground. The narrator accepts this decision as one designed to thwart any potential grave robber. It is also accepted, in the usual reading of the tale, as necessary for the reappearance of Madeline.

Here lies an error, for a Madeline in the vault is as well buried as a Madeline under six feet of earth. In short, Roderick's sister cannot escape her burial place: therefore the living Madeline cannot reappear. The narrator says,

> At the request of Usher, I personally aided him in the arrangements for the temporary entombment. The body having been encoffined, we two alone bore it to its rest. The vault in which we placed it (and which had

"The Dual Hallucination in 'The Fall of the House of Usher'" by John S. Hill. From Southwest Review XLVIII (1963), pp. 396–402. Copyright © 1963 by Southern Methodist University Press. Reprinted by permission of Southwest Review and John S. Hill.

been so long unopened that our torches, half smothered in its oppressive atmosphere, gave us little opportunity for investigation) was small,
damp, and entirely without means of admission for light; . . . a portion
of its floor, and the whole interior of a long archway through which we
reached it, were carefully sheathed with copper. The door, of massive
iron, had been, also, similarly protected. Its immense weight caused an
unusually sharp grating sound, as it moved upon its hinges.

. . . we partially turned aside the yet unscrewed lid of the coffin, and
looked upon the face of the tenant. . . . The disease which had thus
entombed the lady in the maturity of youth, had left, as usual in all
maladies of a strictly cataleptical character, the mockery of a faint blush
upon the bosom and the face, and that suspiciously lingering smile upon
the lip which is so terrible in death. We replaced and screwed down the
lid, and having secured the door of iron, made our way . . . into . . .
the upper portion of the house. [III, 288–89]

These details are important: the air in the vault half smothers the
torches—indicating a lack of sufficient oxygen; the floor of the vault
and the passageway to it are copper covered—making it even more difficult for air to enter; the lid of the coffin is screwed down—Madeline's
body is secured within the coffin; the door is of iron and of immense
weight and is fastened from the outside—it would be impossible to
open it from within, especially if one were weak from illness, left without food, water, and light, and had an insufficient air supply.

It is a week before Madeline reappears.

It is absurd to imagine that Madeline breaks open her coffin, un-
fastens the massive iron door, and goes up into the House. Yet the
usual reading of the story accepts the impossible.

The acceptance relies upon Poe's description of Madeline's body—
the color in her face, the smile lingering about her mouth—and upon
the nature of her illness: cataleptic. Does this description *reveal* that
Madeline has been buried alive? No, it merely *suggests*. This is part of
the reason why the general reading accepts Madeline's return as that of
the real Madeline. I say "part" because it is not all of the reason. The
greater cause for acceptance comes from the narrator himself, for he
too believes the returned Madeline is the real Madeline. He does not
realize that Madeline is an apparition, for by the end of the story he is
insane enough to conjure a hallucination too. The usual reading accepts the madman's view that Madeline is alive; thus Madeline-as-hal-
lucination is overlooked.

To understand why the hallucination is passed over, one must first
consider two of the three principals of the story: Roderick Usher and
the House of Usher itself.

The House of Usher and its companion gloom are described in such phrases as "clouds hung oppressively low," "dreary tract of country," "shades of the evening," "a sense of insufferable gloom," "the bleak walls," "the decayed trees"; "ghastly tree-stems," "vacant and eye-like windows"; "an atmosphere . . . reeked up from the decayed trees," "excessive antiquity," "extensive decay"; "windows . . . inaccessible," "dark draperies," "air of stern, deep, and irredeemable gloom"; also, "a barely perceptible fissure" is indicative of the House of Usher's pending collapse [III, 273–78].

There are only two references to bright light, and both are portentous. Roderick's painting of a vault shows "a flood of intense rays" and, just prior to the appearance of the ghost, bright, unnatural light surrounds the House of Usher [III, 283, 291]. Otherwise, the House and the atmosphere both within and without are so intensely gloomy that, given time, they bear down upon the spirit of the narrator himself, just as they have borne down upon the spirit of Roderick Usher. The dark, depressing atmosphere is indicative of evil, and when the worst happens, the House splits asunder and vanishes into the tarn.

The portrait of Roderick Usher is that of a man going mad. He is the end product of a time-honored race noted for its "peculiar sensibility of temperament." He is also the end product of in-breeding. The line of Usher never branched out; it suffered from a "deficiency . . . of collateral issue, and the consequent undeviating transmission, from sire to son, of the patrimony with the name . . ." [III, 275]. The lack of collateral issue indicates that, more likely than not, Usher cousin married Usher cousin and, to employ a phrase of that time, no new blood was introduced to reinforce the family tree. In such a line of descent strong traits are very often replaced by weaker ones. For instance, Roderick suffers from "an excessive nervous agitation."

> It was . . . a constitutional and a family evil . . . It displayed itself in a host of unnatural sensations. . . . He suffered much from a morbid acuteness of the senses; the most insipid food was alone endurable; he could wear only garments of certain texture; the odours of all flowers were oppressive; his eyes were tortured by even a faint light; and there were but peculiar sounds, and these from stringed instruments, which did not inspire him with horror. [III, 280]

Also, he is bound to the House: "for many years, he had never ventured forth—in regard to an influence . . . his family mansion had . . . obtained over his spirit . . ." [III, 281].

Roderick speaks of " 'this intolerable agitation of soul. . . . I feel that the period will sooner or later arrive when I must abandon life and reason together, in some struggle with the grim phantasm, FEAR' "

[III, 280]. The narrator observes in Roderick "a mind from which darkness, as if an inherent positive quality, poured forth upon all objects in one unceasing radiation of gloom" [III, 280].

Roderick paints, and "there arose out of the pure abstractions which the hypochondriac contrived to throw upon his canvas, an intensity of intolerable awe . . ." [III, 283]. He also plays and sings; one of his "wild fantasias" is the song, "The Haunted Palace," which makes the narrator perceive, "for the first time, a full consciousness on the part of Usher, of the tottering of his lofty reason upon her throne" [III, 284].

He believes in "the sentience of all vegetable things" [III, 286] and connects this belief with the House itself. Thus he can believe that the House has the power to dominate the lives of those within; also, because he believes in the consciousness of the very stones of the House, he can well add another human attribute—possession of a soul—to the House of Usher. The belief that he himself, Madeline, and the House have a common soul is but a short step beyond. Further, he reads such books as Machiavelli's *Belphegor,* Swedenborg's *Heaven and Hell,* Ludwig Holberg's *Subterranean Voyage of Nicholas Klimm,* and Nicolas Eymeric de Gironne's *Directorium Inquisitorum* [III, 287].

Everything attributed to Roderick Usher indicates mental instability: his extreme nervousness, his belief in the sentience of vegetable matter, his fixation about being ruled by the House itself, his wild music, and, most indicative, his fear of fear itself, which is actually fear of his incipient madness. Furthermore, there are the narrator's own observations about Roderick's darkened mind and the narrator's realization that Roderick himself knows he is going insane.

At this point in the tale, Madeline dies. Whatever Roderick does thereafter may be interpreted by the narrator as a deed done in grief. Madeline's is an artistically well-timed death, for it supplies an apparent reason for Roderick's melancholia. Also, and again artistically, it allows Poe to skip over a week's time without giving the reader much additional insight into Roderick. Thus, at the end of the story, although a week has passed, we remember Roderick as he was before: tottering on the brink of insanity. It is only in retrospect that we discover that, during the week, he fell into the abyss.

Here, it must be understood that Roderick had to cross the line into madness, for only this point will serve to explain the ending. In brief, Roderick must be mentally unbalanced if he is to conjure Madeline's ghost, for indeed the hallucination that Madeline returns alive from the grave is but the product of Roderick's mind. The proof of such an interpretation lies in the text.

As observed earlier, Madeline's body has been locked in a coffin which in turn has been locked in a vault. The chamber has an insufficient supply of air, and no food or water is provided, so even if she were not dead, it is improbable she could escape her coffin and, even if she accomplished the improbable, it is impossible that she forced the massive iron door. Also, she would not have lived for a week under the conditions within the tomb. Therefore the question for decision is not whether Madeline really escapes but whether Madeline really is dead at the time when she is buried.

I do not believe Roderick Usher when he cries in terror, " '*We have put her living in the tomb!* '" [III, 296]. That is, I do not accept this as a literal statement; I believe it is what Roderick in his madness thinks he has done.

As has been pointed out, the Ushers and their House have a common soul, and the death of one means death for all. Furthermore, Roderick's statements about the House controlling him show he is aware of this. If so, is he willingly going to murder his sister? And we must not forget the narrator: he notices the apparent bloom on her cheek; if he has the slightest idea that Madeline might be in a cataleptic fit instead of being dead, will he help bury her alive? Obviously not. The shadowy idea that Madeline might be alive in her coffin leads to such self-contradictory statements as this one by Edward H. Davidson: "his twin sister, a part of him, he tries to destroy because her removal might free him from a painful physical life; but he knows that as soon as she dies, he dies too; thus he tries to bury her alive." [1]

If Roderick believes he will die when Madeline dies, why ensure her death by burying her alive? Would not Roderick do all within his power to prolong her life? Certainly he would. But this is not the major point of the story. Had Poe written merely of Roderick-Madeline-House as a single soul, he could have accomplished his purpose by having Roderick drop dead after entombing Madeline. But Poe sought to do more. He wished to write a tale about madness, and he succeeded —doubly well.

Madeline's body is interred within the House for two reasons: to prevent body snatchers from digging up her corpse and to permit Roderick to imagine he hears her struggling to escape from her tomb. If she were buried in the remote family plot, it would be absurd to assume he imagined he heard her digging through the earth.

After the interment, the narrator records that,

> And now, some days of bitter grief having elapsed, an observable change came over the features of the mental disorder of my friend. His ordinary manner had vanished. . . . He roamed from chamber to cham-

[1] "Introduction," *Selected Writings of Edgar Allan Poe* (Boston: Houghton Mifflin Co., 1956), xvi.

ber with hurried, unequal, and objectless step. . . . There were times, indeed, when I thought his unceasingly agitated mind was labouring with some oppressive secret, to divulge which he struggled for the necessary courage. At times, again, I was obliged to resolve all into the mere inexplicable vagaries of madness, for I beheld him gazing upon vacancy for long hours, in an attitude of the profoundest attention, as if listening to some imaginary sound. [III, 289]

One of Roderick Usher's abnormalities is an acute auditory sense; couple this fact with the statement that a "favorite volume" was the *Directorium Inquisitorum*; blend these two facts with a third, supplied by the narrator: Roderick is mad. The result is an insane man whose interest in torture might well make him imagine he had perpetrated one of the most fiendish of tortures—burying someone alive. And this insane man, if he possessed very acute hearing, might well listen for the sounds which would confirm what his unbalanced mind set forth as a fact. In short, Roderick hears the sounds from below because he *wants* to hear them, and a shattered mind can hear whatever it wishes.

The insane belief that Madeline lives is the "oppressive secret" Roderick vainly struggles to reveal. He thinks that if Madeline, the House, and he himself have a common soul, they will have a common death. Yet he is alive. Thus, reasons his unbalanced mind, Madeline must be alive too. He cannot tell his friend, however, simply because he cannot yet admit to burying her alive. Later, under the pressure of extreme terror, he will reveal the deed.

One night, a week after Madeline's burial, Roderick enters the narrator's room. Roderick has "a species of mad hilarity in his eyes—an evidently restrained *hysteria* in his whole demeanour" [III, 291]. He is greatly upset by a physical phenomenon—the ghostly light about the House—and the narrator undertakes to soothe him by reading aloud.

Roderick is prepared to hear certain sounds. When the narrator reads, " 'the noise of the dry and hollow-sounding wood alarumed and reverberated throughout the forest,' " there is heard "the echo . . . of the very cracking and ripping sound which Sir Launcelot had so particularly described." When he reads, " 'a shriek so horrid and harsh,' " there is heard an "unusual screaming or grating sound—," and when he reads, " 'a mighty great and terrible ringing sound,' " there is heard "a distinct, hollow, metallic, and clangorous, yet apparently muffled reverberation" [III, 293–95].

As for Roderick, his uncertain reason is responding to the stimuli of the sounds described in the novel. As he sits, "his eyes were bent fixedly before him, and throughout his whole countenance there reigned a stony rigidity . . . he spoke in a low, hurried, and gibbering murmur . . ." He mutters, " 'Long—long—long—many minutes, many hours, many days, have I heard it—yet . . . I *dared* not speak! *We have put her living in the tomb!'* " (Poe's italics.) As his mind rushes further beyond the edge of reason, he cries out, " 'Will she not be here anon? Is she not hurrying to upbraid me for my haste? Have I not heard her footsteps on the stair? Do I not distinguish that heavy and horrible beating of her heart?' " [III, 295–96].

His aberrant mind may choose what it wishes to believe, for in unreality are all things real. Thus he assumes that Madeline is alive and is approaching. It is but a short step to conjure a hallucination; this Roderick does when the doors open: he sees Madeline. She falls upon him, and he dies.

Roderick, believing he has fiendishly tortured his sister, is prepared to have her take revenge upon him. His hallucination, then, is not only the product of an erratic mind but of a wish to die himself. But such is madness.

To realize that Poe went even beyond this point is to pay tribute to his genius as a craftsman and as an imaginative writer. For his goal in this tale—a goal he reached—is not just to show Roderick going insane but to show also the narrator's own descent into madness.

In the first part of the story, the narrator is virtually overwhelmed by the gloom of the House of Usher. His description, which is a record of his own impressions, includes such modifiers as "oppressively," "insufferable," "dark," and "decayed." He has an acute imagination; he records that:

> I had so worked upon my imagination as really to believe that about the whole mansion and domain there hung an atmosphere which . . . had reeked up from the decayed trees . . . [III, 276]

By the time Madeline had been interred, the narrator has so succumbed to the gloom of the House of Usher that he reports, "It was no wonder that his condition terrified—that it infected me. *I felt creeping upon me, by slow yet certain degrees, the wild influences of his own fantastic yet impressive superstitions*" [III, 289–90; italics supplied].

I underscore this sentence because it is the first major key to understanding the narrator's descent into madness. The narrator feels himself sinking into Roderick's black world, yet still is rational enough to label it all as "superstitions." Still he admits he is entering Roderick's wild world by "slow yet certain" degrees. These two sentences end a paragraph. The next paragraph begins the final section of the tale. The narrator reports hearing "certain low and indefinite sounds which came . . . I knew not whence" [III, 290]. Then Roderick enters, and the narrator reads to him. And when the sounds come from down within the House, the narrator hears them too. This shows he has already entered Roderick's sphere; he has gone mad himself.

Another item of proof, if another be needed, occurs when Roderick shouts, " *'We have put her living in the tomb!'* " After he says he has heard Madeline ascending the stairs, he shouts, " 'MADMAN!'—here he sprang furiously to his feet, and shrieked out his syllables, as if in the effort he were giving up his soul—'MADMAN! I TELL YOU THAT SHE NOW STANDS WITHOUT THE DOOR!' " [III, 296].

Roderick is addressing the narrator. He includes him when he says "we" buried her, and he is speaking directly to the narrator when twice he shouts "MADMAN!" When Roderick calls his companion insane, he provides the second major key to understanding the narrator's state of mind.

The third major key is the hallucination, which has been so long overlooked. The usual reading accepts Madeline as a living being because of the narrator's presence: it is assumed that because *he* sees Madeline she must be alive. The truth lies to the contrary: since the facts prove Madeline is dead, she must reappear strictly as a hallucination. And the narrator not only sees the apparition, he flees from it as well.

This is Poe's grand achievement in "The Fall of the House of Usher": he not only creates one man, Roderick, going mad, but creates two; he not only creates one man who conjures a hallucination, but he has the narrator cross over into Roderick's world so that he too sees it. Thus, through the dual hallucination, Poe adds a new dimension to the portrayal of madness.

Poe's "Ligeia" and the English Romantics

by Clark Griffith

More than any of his major American contemporaries, Edgar Allan Poe shifted facilely and readily from one vein of prose fiction directly into another. There simply were no well-defined stages in Poe's writing, no set periods during which he concentrated exclusively upon some particular aspect of his prose material. Even the early, abortive Folio Club project was designed for a combination of humorous sketches and Gothic tales. And later as Poe's interests broadened to include satire, philosophy, and ratiocinative themes, he proved quite capable of composing, all within the space of a few months, a characteristic horror story, a burlesque, an analytical tale, and a metaphysical dialogue.

Yet it is a curious fact that critical studies of Poe regularly ignore the chronological pattern of his work and emphasize instead its similarities according to type. One can find a dozen worth-while books or essays in which scattered examples of Poe's fiction, individual pieces done ten or fifteen years apart, are lumped together in breathlessly neat categories. But one looks in vain for an interpreter who acknowledges that, however apparently different the actual texts may be, what Poe wrote in a given June was just possibly influenced by—was somehow interrelated with—what he had already written in the preceding May. The results of this overcompartmentalized approach are, I think, lamentable. Not only does study always by type but never by time destroy all sense of the continuity in Poe's writing. Much more seriously, it completely blinds us to whatever possibility there is that his scrambled order of composition, his easy hopping from genre to genre, may sometimes have been shrewdly purposeful—and may sometimes be most astonishingly revealing.

By way then of exploring certain potentialities latent in a chronological rather than typal investigation of Poe, let us consider "Ligeia"

"Poe's 'Ligeia' and the English Romantics" by *Clark Griffith*. From University of Toronto Quarterly *XXIV (1954), pp. 8–13, 16–25. Copyright © 1954 by University of Toronto Press. Reprinted by permission of University of Toronto Press and Clark Griffith.*

(1838). . . . "Ligeia" *is* what perceptive critics ranging from Philip Pendleton Cooke to Allen Tate have always called it, a gripping horror story, successfully rescued from the triteness of its kind by Poe's painstaking craftsmanship. It is, to be sure; and yet as one reads and re-reads the narrative, certain troublesome features persistently intrude. Problems of tone and symbolism, of characterization and, above all, of style, they never for a moment suggest that "Ligeia" is not a piece of Gothic fiction. . . . What they do imply is that close and searching scrutiny should make us the more wary of accepting it as simply a tale of terror, and as a text in which Gothic devices constitute the sole level of meaning. . . .

The first version of "Ligeia" appeared in the September, 1838, issue of the *American Museum of Literature and the Arts.* During this same year, Poe published only two other prose pieces, "Siope—A Fable," written (probably sometime late in 1837) for the January *Baltimore Book,* and "Psyche Zenobia," a burlesque which also appeared in the *American Museum,* just two months after "Ligeia." Both are obvious satires; and although they approach them quite differently, both satirize identical subjects . . .[1]

"Siope" [is] a ruthless parody of Transcendentalism; "Psyche Zenobia," a merciless burlesque of Transcendental and Gothic writing; and between them [stands] the "Ligeia." At first glance, certainly, such a combination appears to do little more than underscore both the variety and the incredible unevenness in Poe's creative methods. Reading "Ligeia" as a straightforward tale of terror and turning then to the satires, one is readily persuaded that Poe himself drifted aimlessly— somewhat too aimlessly—from arrant nonsense into fiction of a high order into a realm of petty drivel, and that under the circumstances this is the only plausible deduction. Still, our initial examination of "Ligeia" unearthed several problems which the conventional approach did not seem fitted to solve. And when, with these matters brought to the foreground, the three pieces are read in the order of their publication, parallels or unexpected possibilities for parallels abruptly crystallize.

For one thing, it quickly becomes apparent that both "Siope" with its Gothic background plus its inarguable irony and "Psyche Zenobia"

---

[1] Texts of the two pieces first appeared in *The Baltimore Book* (1838), pp. 79–85, and *American Museum of Literature and the Arts* I (November, 1838), pp. 301–10. When reprinted in *Tales of the Grotesque and Arabesque* (1840), the titles changed to "Silence—A Fable" and "The Signora Zenobia." When reprinted in *The Broadway Journal* (July 12, 1845), the latter title changed again, to "How to Write a Blackwood Article." See II, 220–24, 269–82.—ED.

with its strange synthesis of *bizarrerie* and *intensity* ought to make us doubly sceptical of another tale of terror which contains any sort of questionable leavening. If Poe could play a trick once, he could likewise perform it twice; if he could theorize about a combination of Gothic *clichés* and Transcendental gibberish, he could also put theory into practice. But this is far from being all. "Siope" with its lush prose and "Psyche Zenobia" with its sardonic commentary on philosophical styles to be emphasized in terrifying situations should prompt us to look cautiously at other passages where Poe's language is a shade too full, a trace too mystical or metaphysical. And there is more. Just as "Siope" might well put us on guard for other references to opium dreams and Transcendentalism, just so "Psyche Zenobia" should alert us to another text in which Transcendentalism, Germany, England, indeed a kind of international motif figure large though ambiguously. And still more. Both implicitly and explicitly "Ligeia" *does* share qualities of the satires. Slight though it is, the allegorical method in "Psyche Zenobia" reminds us that "Ligeia" too is allegory. The pursuits ascribed to the lady Ligeia prefigure Mr. Blackwood's precepts. In "Ligeia" there are certain words and phrases which relate backward to "Siope," look ahead to "Psyche Zenobia."

. . . The burlesques published before and after "Ligeia" illuminate certain difficult aspects of "Ligeia" precisely because "Ligeia" is partly burlesque. Like "Siope," its predecessor, it combines Gothic overplot with satiric underside. Full of terror and sentiment but also of metaphysics and erudition, it duplicates the ideal horror story delineated in "Psyche Zenobia," its sequel. It is, in a word, an allegory of terror, almost perfectly co-ordinated with the subtlest of allegorized jests. . . .

In the surface-allegory, the lady Ligeia stands for mystery and madness, for an inflexible will to live, and for symbolic unreason. In the allegorized jest, her meanings are tailored to exemplify the mystery of a particular form of madness.

She was of a German background. Her studies "were more than all else adapted to deaden impressions of the outward world." The narrator felt her "rare learning" and "enthralling eloquence" creep into his heart by paces "steadily and stealthily progressive." Often, he remained unaware of her presence except as a "low sweet voice" drifting through his closed study. Ligeia's beauty "was the radiance of an opium dream"; and—in words lifted directly out of "Siope"—it was a vision more wildly divine "than the phantasies which hovered about the slumbering souls of the daughters of Delos." Additionally, her physical appearance shared the luxuriant grace of the Hebrews and the majestic spirituality of the Greeks [II, 249].

Ligeia's eyes were the seat of a profound spirituality. During moments of "intense excitement," the "luminous orbs" acquired a beauty wholly distinct "from the formation, or the color, or the brilliancy of the features." At such times, their *"expression"* was of supreme importance, for it became rich with a metaphysical allusiveness, reflected back to the narrator "the beauty of beings either above or apart from the earth." Yet there was something immoderately singular about Ligeia's *"expression."* Ineffable and inscrutable, it resembled Mr. Blackwood's "tone mystic," hinting much but asserting nothing. Even for the narrator, who sought after complete understanding, the *"expression"* represented a "word of no meaning"; like *Silence* ("which is the merest word of all"), *"expression"* was a "vast latitude of mere sound [behind which] we entrench our ignorance of so much of the spiritual." But if Ligeia's profoundest glances were themselves unknowable, they did reproduce faint traces of their spirituality in an endless circle of known analogies —in "the commonest objects of the universe" and in "many existences in the material world" [II, 250–52].

Ligeia's intellect was immense. An *"intensity* in thought" set her apart from all others; and her learning, "gigantic" and "astounding," fanned out in every direction, came at last to encompass every conceivable area of knowledge. She was deeply proficient "in the classical tongues" and in all the "modern dialects of Europe." (Recall how the benefits of " 'French, Spanish, Italian, German, Latin, and Greek' " were to be impressed upon Psyche Zenobia.) Her mastery extended over all "the most admired, because simply the most abstruse of the boasted erudition of the academy." (" 'Talk of the academy and the lyceum,' " Psyche Zenobia would soon be counselled.) With astonishing ease, she traversed "*all* the wide areas of moral, natural, and mathematical science." (Psyche Zenobia was to hear much of Fichte, Kant, and Bossarion.) She guided the narrator, a child by contrast, through the "chaotic world of metaphysical investigation." (The schools Italic and Ionic, the terms *a priori* and *a posteriori* were to be important parts of Psyche Zenobia's education.) And then comes the key comment which lends both point and purpose to this altogether ludicrous account of Ligeia. Her "presence, her readings alone, rendered vividly luminous the many mysteries of . . . transcendentalism" [II, 253–54]. Ligeia was a Transcendentalist.

She symbolizes, in sober fact, the very incarnation of German idealism, German Transcendentalism provided with an allegorical form. First suggested by her nationality and mystical behaviour and subjectivistic studies, her role in the satire is further betrayed by the meaningless meaning of her strangely metaphysical eyes. It is reemphasized by her spiritual glances, unintelligible except for their reappearance in material existences. It is rounded out by her "intensities," her personification of just the qualities Psyche Zenobia would presently be urged to cultivate, her elucidation of Transcendental mysteries. If, however, additional evidence seems desirable, it can easily be drawn from the narrator's attitude toward and his relationship with Ligeia.

In the Gothic overplot, the narrator is pictured as a psychopath, as a bereaved husband, and as the recording consciousness, shattered by the anomalies it perceives. In the satiric underside of "Ligeia," his lunacy becomes the lunacy of a confirmed "Crazyite."

The narrator was Ligeia's student in the sense that the dark lady was his teacher. He was a student of Ligeia in the sense that she represented the object of his studies. As the "unfathomable meaning of [Ligeia's] glance" sank deeply into his soul, the narrator longed for larger understanding. Relentlessly, he pondered her expression. Throughout the "whole of a midsummer night," he "struggled to fathom it." What was it, he never wearied of asking himself, "What was it—that something more profound than the well of Democritus—which lay far within the pupils of my beloved? What *was* it? . . . Those eyes! those large, those shining, those divine orbs!" [II, 251–52]. But when no response was forthcoming, he temporarily abandoned all hopes for complete comprehension, and contented himself with "discovering in the commonest objects of the universe, a circle of analogies to that expression." He recognized something of its spirituality in the

> survey of a rapidly growing vine—in the contemplation of a moth, a butterfly, a chrysalis, a stream of running water . . . in the ocean, in the falling of a meteor . . . in the glances of unusually aged people . . . [in] one or two stars . . . [in] certain sounds from stringed instruments . . . [in] passages from books . . . in a volume of Joseph Glanvill . . .: 'And the will therein lieth, which dieth not. Who knoweth the mysteries of the will, with its vigor? For God is but a great will pervading all things by nature of its intentness. Man doth not yield him to the angels utterly, save only through the weakness of his feeble will.' [II, 253–54]

Of the dozen or so items in this list, only one—the so-called Glanvill quotation—bears directly upon the overplot. For the rest, they simply suggest that Poe is slyly mocking Ligeia's spiritual depths by comparing them to an assortment of oddly incongruous details, by describing them in prose very like the "tone heterogenous." And opening up this possibility, they instantly remind one of the Transcendentalists who were likewise glimpsing spiritual analogues in the "commonest objects of the universe," in such "'pertinent and pretty'" places as nature, clothes-symbols, and the works of German literature.

For the narrator, Ligeia posed an unsolved metaphysical riddle. But mystified and entranced by her rare learning, he confidently assumed that she herself would ultimately unravel the puzzle which she herself symbolized. Humbly aware of her "infinite supremacy," he pursued like an eager child the obscure import of her teachings. And, as he expresses it,

> With how vast a triumph—with how vivid a delight—with how much of all that is ethereal in hope—did I *feel,* as she bent over me, in studies but little sought for—but less known that delicious vista by slow but very perceptible degrees expanding before me, down whose long, gorgeous, and all untrodden path I might at length pass onward to the goal of a wisdom too divinely precious not to be forbidden. [II, 254]

Then, as before, there comes the final comment, justifying this fantastic, this almost obscene overwriting. At the foot of the path lay full mastery of the "many mysteries of the transcendentalism" in which the narrator was immersed. By first portraying himself as the student of Ligeia and next as the student of Transcendentalism, by passing at once from the many mysteries of Ligeia to the many mysteries of Transcendentalism, Poe's spokesman has confirmed the dark lady's place in the satire—and thereby disclosed his own.

Actually two things are fundamentally dubious about the narrator's reference to Transcendental pursuits. Although Poe's tales of terror frequently picture the human mind in its gradual advance upon esoteric knowledge, the exact nature of the new discovery is seldom, if ever, divulged. In "Ms. Found in a Bottle" or "The Fall of the House of Usher," no character can even visualize, much less define, the awful mysteries for which he is compelled to search; their vagueness is an indispensable adjunct to the supernaturalism in the story. Here, by contrast, the object of the intellectual quest is not merely named. It is explicitly embodied in another character and, what is yet more suspect, it is given the selfsame label Poe had already flayed once and would flay again in the year 1838. Surely, these facts are of overriding significance: surely, they contribute all the proof needed to identify the narrator as a prototype of Poe's favourite whipping-boy, the Transcendentalist who speaks the language of a *Blackwood's intensity,* who looks into the "nature of affairs a very great deal farther than anybody else," and whose intellectual pretensions are bolstered by gleamings from the German.

Ligeia died; and her death, her fierce struggles, and grim wrestlings with the shadow belong to the Gothic overplot. The narrator's reaction, however, is a different matter. Recounting Ligeia's fatal illness, he makes it clear that his chief bereavement was the loss of her informing glances. When her eyes, at once the symbol of the Transcendental puzzle and the avenue to its resolution, shone "less and less frequently upon the pages over which [he] pored," the narrator's despair knew no bounds. Wanting the "radiant luster" of those eyes, he cries in an agony of grief, "letters, lambent and golden, grew duller than Saturnian lead" [II, 254]. Not simply letters, but golden letters; this, as it happens, is the initial allusion to gold, one of the two basic colours in Poe's allegory.

Other gold-images quickly accumulate once the narrator arrives in England. England itself is "fair." Rowena Trevanion of Tremaine is "fair-haired." The accoutrements of the narrator's English estate include gold carpets, golden candelabra, gold tapestries and ottomans, chains and pendants of solid gold. Yet despite the garish splendour of all these objects, none are permitted to shine with a pure golden radiance. Across one wall of the apartment where they were located and where the narrator dwelt with Rowena, there ran a single window-pane. It was "an immense sheet of unbroken glass . . . and tinted of a leaden hue, so that the rays of either sun or moon, passing through it, fell with a ghastly luster on the objects within" [II, 259]. Now there is, to be sure, nothing inherently peculiar in such a window; it is sinister-looking and blends sufficiently well into the Gothic backdrop. Nevertheless, its appearance in this context does balance out a curious parallel. In effect, Poe has transferred to Rowena and to the English *mise en scène* the same leaden dullness which overspread the golden letters of Transcendentalism when the German Ligeia could no longer gloss and enrich their inmost meanings.

As we have noticed, several features connected with the abbey, with Rowena, and with the narrator's behaviour in fair England are not readily assimilable into the surface allegory. But if, as seems likely, Poe's colour scheme is less a matter of coincidence than of malicious design, these apparent inanities merge in the allegorized satire and become the cream of the jest.

The abbey was situated in one of "the wildest and least frequented portions of fair England," in a region notoriously "remote and unsocial." Surrounded by "gloomy" and "dreary grandeur," overhung with "mossy" ruin, "aged vine," and "verdant decay," the external building faced upon a "savage domain." Within, were "melancholy and time-honored memories," castellated turrets, ceilings "excessively lofty, vaulted, and elaborately fretted with the wildest and most grotesque specimens of a semi-Gothic, semi-druidical device" [II, 258–59]. Clearly enough, this reads much like a typical Poe setting. But the trouble is that it typifies, almost too perfectly, the whole of an intellectual-aesthetic era as well. Swamped by a welter of Romantic *clichés* and perceiving how each is quite uncharacteristically pinned down to a specific geographical locale, we suspect that the English abbey, like the

lady Ligeia and Mr. Blackwood's editorial rooms, is less a traditional
Poe-symbol than a merely traditional symbol, exposed here to Poe's
acid parody. The abbey could be—and, in point of fact, there is abun-
dant evidence for stating it is—a take-off on Scott's scenic effects, similarly, it could be interpreted as Poe's caricature of the desolate land-
scape at Craigenputtock or of the Lake Country and the "violet by the
mossy stone."

Filling any or all of these roles, the abbey is brilliantly suited to its
principal English occupant, the lady Rowena Trevanion of Tremaine.
With her name drawn equally out of *Ivanhoe* and "Christabel,"
Rowena, we may fairly assume, is the living incarnation of English
Romanticism, English Romantic—or English Transcendental—
thought cloaked in allegorical trappings. Yet in the narrator's view,
the lady of Tremaine was as destitute of Ligeia's miraculous insights
as of her stupendous learning and oracular gibberish. Conventional
and dull, the blond was simply another of those golden objects over-
cast by the leaden-grey window. Only in a moment "of his mental
alienation" did she seem to the narrator to be a fit "successor of the
unforgotten Ligeia"; soon he came to loathe her "with a hatred be-
longing more to demon than to man" [II, 259, 261]. Rowena, in short,
symbolizes an impoverished English Romanticism, as yet "unspiritual-
ized" by German cant. Consequently, she represents but a shallow pre-
tense of Romanticism; and—on this point the text is admirably plain
—it is a part of Poe's joke to make her Romantic in nothing save her
borrowed name.

Despising Rowena, abandoning himself to orgies of grief, the narrator increasingly revelled "(oh with what intensity of regret)" in recollections of Ligeia's "purity, of her wisdom, of her lofty, her ethereal
nature." He perpetuated her memory in the lavish *décor* of his cham-
bers. Appropriately, he invoked her spirit in nature, calling "aloud
upon her name . . . among the sheltered recesses of the glens." Chiefly,
however, he sought to recover her mystical being in the wild hallucina-
tions engendered by opium. From the outset, we observed, he identified
Ligeia's transcendent beauty with an opium dream, and early betrayed
something of Poe's satiric intent by describing her in terms first used in
"Siope." Now when his spirit most burned to unite with "all the fires
of [Ligeia's] own," he was habitually fettered "in the shackles of the
drug." As the author of *Confessions of an Opium-Eater* (in Poe's mind,
Coleridge) deplored the dearth of English philosophy and boasted in
the same breath of his opium feats and wide readings from the German, so Poe's narrator, contemptuous of the English Rowena, gave
himself up to drugged visions of the German Ligeia. The very decora-
tions, where emblems of Ligeia's dark spirituality were scattered across

Rowena's grey-gold dullness, took their "colouring from [his] dreams."
Excited by opium, he shrieked Ligeia's name "during the silences of the
night." In a drugged frenzy, he glimpsed her mystical shadow, and felt
his "whole soul was awakened within." Opium and Ligeia were inseparable; together with nature, the narcotic became a means of restor-
ing the dark lady "to the pathways she had abandoned upon earth"
[II, 261].

But there is, to repeat, no satisfactory reason why the narrator's ad-
diction should appear in the Gothic overplot. Inevitably, it weakens
the climax of the tale, suggesting that what the narrator finally beholds
is more delusion than objective circumstance. Hence it goes far toward
vitiating the drama of Ligeia's restoration—unless, of course, that
restoration is susceptible to a second interpretation.

When Poe's friend and critic Philip Pendleton Cooke examined the
first published version of "Ligeia," he complained of only one major
defect. For the sake of fuller credibility, he insisted, the conclusion
should have been somewhat modified. The completed transition from
Rowena to Ligeia was a "violation of the ghostly proprieties"; a reader
would be shocked into unbelief upon discovering how a "wandering
essence . . . could, *in quickening the body of the Lady Rowena* (such
is the idea) become suddenly the visible, bodily, Ligeia." Poe made
great show of agreeing. "Touching Ligeia," he replied, "you are right
—all right—throughout. . . . I should have intimated that the *will*
did not perfect its intention—there should have been a relapse—a final
one—and Ligeia should be at length entombed as Rowena—the bodily
alterations having gradually faded away." [2] Yet the fact remains that
twice during the next seven years "Ligeia" underwent revisions extensive and slight; and on both occasions Poe left essentially unchanged
the ending for which he had so profusely apologized. Did he retain the
objectionable climax because, as he rather lamely (and for that matter,
rather inaccurately) told Cooke, it differentiated between "Ligeia" and
the earlier "Morella"? Or did he retain it because, hugely enjoying the
second, secret meaning of his "wandering essence," he recognized that
Ligeia's bodily conquest of Rowena was absolutely necessary for the
satire? In view of all that has gone before and in terms of the conclusion itself, the latter alternative seems considerably more plausible.

For what, in its largest sense, does the "ghostly" transformation in
"Ligeia" signify? Why, nothing less, really, than a dramatic enactment
of what would become one of the most comic sections of "Psyche
Zenobia." To the Signora—fretting because her Romantic compatriots
lacked "profundity . . . reading . . . metaphysics . . . spirituality

---

[2] [XVII, 50]; *Letters*, II, 110.

. . . cant . . . with a capital K," fretting because "there was no investigation of first causes, first principles . . . no attention paid to that
great point the 'fitness of things' "—to this sorely tried lady, Mr. Blackwood would offer sage words of wisdom. Write many languages. Master
metaphysics. Talk of the academy. Bring in the words *a priori* and *a
posteriori*. Stress the Germans; above all, stress the Germans. Abuse
Locke, but praise Fichte, Schelling and Kant. Make *The Sorrows of
Werther* a by-word. Collectively, these are the pomposities which will
reanimate the deadest of Romanticisms. Since it is Mr. Blackwood who
compiles them, they are, manifestly, the generating root of English
Romanticism itself. Symbolized in the lady Ligeia, they constitute the
"chronic disease" and the "distemper of fancy" which topple Rowena's
reason "from her throne." In turn, they become the vital forces which
rejuvenate Rowena, dispel her clammy pallor, quicken her into new
life—but re-shape her until she is unrecognizable except as Ligeia.

Here, then, at least, shrieks the narrator when his long vigil has
been rewarded: "Here, then, at least . . . can I never—can I never be
mistaken—these are the full, and the black, and the wild eyes of the
lady—of the lady Ligeia" [II, 268]. At the end, it is Ligeia's mystical
expression which prevails. Reflecting a metaphysical beauty, discerni-
ble in nature and dreams, pondered by the student of Transcendentalism, this "vast latitude of mere sound" is Ligeia's link with German
idealism. And now, the "word of no meaning" has left its ineffaceable
stamp upon Rowena. In the allegorized jest, therefore, qualities fundamentally German do indeed take primacy over properties basically
English. For Poe has compounded terror with satire, and the triumph
of German sources over an English Romanticism, hopelessly uninspired
without them, could hardly be more complete.

"Ligeia" and Its Critics:
A Plea for Literalism

by John Lauber

In the past twenty years a kind of small-scale *Turn of the Screw* controversy has developed over the interpretation of Poe's "Ligeia." The issues are strikingly similar. In each work a narrator describes supernatural events, in each the traditional view has been to take the supernatural occurrences at face value, ascribing to them an equal reality with the other happenings of the story, and in each case this literal reading has been questioned by critics who assert that the narrator's statements must be accepted only with considerable qualification and that his accounts of the supernatural proceed either from self-delusion or deliberate lying. The arguments were summarized and the traditional view was ably reasserted by James Schroeter in 1961,[1] but discussion has continued. The basic question about "Ligeia," then, is whether the narrator's word should be trusted, whether he is to be considered as a reliable or unreliable reporter of events. Critics who doubt the narrator necessarily believe that he himself murdered Rowena, his second wife, and that the "revivification" of Ligeia is a hallucination. (Skepticism has been carried even further by Stovall, who suggests that Ligeia never existed at all, but was merely a figment of the narrator's disordered imagination.)[2] Absolute certainty is impossible in such matters, but the critic may hope to establish a reasonable probability. In the case of "Ligeia," the weight of the evidence strongly supports a literal reading.

The quotation from Glanvill, concluding "Man doth not yield himself to the angels, nor unto death utterly, save only through the weak-

---

"'Ligeia' and Its Critics: A Plea for Literalism" by John Lauber. From Studies in Short Fiction *IV (1966), pp. 28–32. Copyright © 1966 by Newberry College. Reprinted by permission of* Studies in Short Fiction.

[1] James Schroeter, "A Misreading of Poe's 'Ligeia,'" *PMLA*, LXXVI (September 1961), 397–406.

[2] Floyd Stovall, "The Conscious Art of Edgar Allan Poe," *College English*, XXIV (March 1963), 417–421 [Reprinted in *TCV*, pp. 172–78].

ness of his feeble will" [II, 248] should be decisive in itself, as Schroeter points out. Its position as epigraph indicates that it announces the major theme—the power of the human will and its capacity to triumph over death. It is a theme that can exist only within the context of a literal reading. This explicit statement is reinforced when it is twice repeated by the dying Ligeia [II, 257–58]. Unless the events of the story are "real," the Glanvill quotation serves no purpose. It is not likely that Poe, who wrote in his review of Hawthorne's *Twice-Told Tales* that once an author determines the effect he wishes his story to create, "If his very initial sentence tends not to the outbringing of this effect, then he has failed in his first step. In the whole composition there should be no word written, of which the tendency, direct or indirect, is not to the one pre-established design" [XI, 108], should have indulged in pointless mystification by choosing an epigraph that would inevitably misdirect the reader, and then compound his error by repeating the quotation twice at a crucial moment of his tale.

If one doubts the narrator's word, it follows that the narrator must be insane and that the true action of the story is of a "journey into madness." [3] Madness may be granted but does not necessarily invalidate his testimony. Poe's comment in "Eleanora" is relevant:". . . the question is not yet settled—whether madness is or is not the loftiest intelligence —whether much that is glorious, whether all that is profound—does not spring from disease of thought—from moods of mind, exalted at the expense of the general intellect" [IV, 236]. The narrator's madness need not mean that he is incapable of reporting accurately what he has perceived, but rather that he may be capable of perceiving realities beyond the dull commonplaces of normal life. The vagueness of his recollection of Ligeia's background is no reason for doubting his word. It is explained that his memory has failed as a consequence of the terrifying experience he has endured, and in any case such vagueness is typical of Poe. If it provides a reason for doubting the existence of Ligeia, then we should logically doubt the existence of the narrator as well. At least we have a name for Ligeia!

In the revivification scene, nothing suggests that the narrator himself is guilty of murder and that the apparent revival of Ligeia is an insane delusion. When the mysterious ruby drops seem to fall from nowhere into Rowena's medicine, Poe gives no hint that the narrator has in fact poisoned his wife. Instead, Poe allows the reader to choose between accepting the reality and supernatural origin of the happening, or ascribing it to a "vivid imagination, rendered morbidly active by the

[3] James W. Gargano, "Poe's 'Ligeia': Dream and Destruction," *College English*, XXIII (February 1962), p. 38.

terror of the lady, by the opium, and by the hour" [II, 263–64]. The context, of course, points to the first alternative. When the figure of Rowena-Ligeia rises from the death-bed, the careful mention of its height, raven-black hair, and large eyes is surely intended to provide the clinching physical details that momentarily persuade us that the impossible has occurred.

The use of an unreliable narrator does not seem to be characteristic of Poe. (When, in "The Spectacles," he does employ such a narrator, he underlines the fact so heavily at the outset that no reader could miss the point.) The effects for which he worked were usually single and intense, and would only have been blurred by doubts as to whether, or exactly how far, the narrator's word could be trusted. It might be added that while we should not uncritically identify Poe with his narrators, neither does he ordinarily make any very significant effort to individualize them. In short, Poe was not James, and his techniques and his artistic concerns were widely different.

External evidence is also available. There is the parallel of "Morella," in which a mother's spirit possesses the body of her daughter. No critic has yet questioned the reliability of its narrator, and "Morella" at least shows that Poe was capable of seriously presenting a situation similar to that of "Ligeia" and expecting his readers to accept it. More importantly, we have Poe's own statement of his intention, in a letter to a friend written about a year after the publication of "Ligeia." "I should have intimated," wrote Poe, "that the will did not perfect its intention—there should have been a relapse—a final one—and Ligeia (who had only succeeded in so much as to convey an idea of the truth to the narrator) should be at length entombed as Rowena—the bodily alterations having gradually faded away." [4] We need not be concerned with the alternative conclusion Poe suggests—the story he actually wrote is the proper object of criticism—but the quotation proves his intention. The "truth" referred to can mean only that Ligeia's spirit had at least temporarily possessed the body of Rowena. The "will" must be the will of Ligeia, which had achieved, for a moment, its conquest of death.

The motives for these interpretations seem clear enough—critics have disliked the story Poe wrote. Living in a post-Romantic age, they have found themselves "irritated or bewildered by its intensity of expression, emphasis on the supernatural, and assumption that 'knowledge' and 'will' are infinitely perfectible." [5] Consequently they have tried to create a new work more in accord with contemporary values

[4] Quoted in Arthur H. Quinn, *Edgar Allan Poe: A Critical Biography* (New York, 1941), p. 271.

[5] Schroeter, p. 398.

and standards of taste. To take the story literally, it is suggested, "is perforce to maintain a straight face in the presence of an admittedly puerile and shabby Gothicism." [6] It is taken for granted that Poe "loathed the Gothic grotesquerie in which he found himself involved," [7] no doubt because the modern critic would loathe it. In a reaction, itself desirable, against the tendency to treat the tales as diagnostic materials to be used in the psychoanalysis of the author, Stovall asserts that Poe's work "was the product of a healthy and alert intelligence," [8] but appears to believe that such an intelligence could not possibly require acceptance of the supernatural, so that all such elements must be rationalized away. Poe's rhetoric, with its polysyllabic diction, its lurid imagery, its constant overstatement and underlining of the point (often literally, by the use of italics) is antipathetic to the modern taste, and it is presumed that therefore it was also antipathetic to Poe and that he employed it in order to characterize his deranged narrators.

None of these contentions will hold. It would be difficult to find proof anywhere in Poe's writings that he "loathed" the "Gothic grotesquerie" that appears in so much of his work; on the contrary, all the evidence suggests that it fascinated him. The supernatural has nearly disappeared from contemporary literature, but surely it is a kind of temporal provincialism to assume that therefore a writer of the mid-nineteenth century could not have made serious use of it. As for the style, it is essentially the same in "Ligeia" and in "The Masque of the Red Death," in which the author writes in his own person rather than through the medium of a narrator. It is necessary to the effect of the more "Gothic" tales. If one objects to what Auden has called, in his introduction to the Rinehart Poe, the "operatic prose and décor" of the tales, then one is rejecting the tales themselves, for as Auden continues, Poe's "heroes cannot exist except operatically." Such a rejection could be defended, but the critic should be aware of what he is doing, rather than disguising his rejection as a reinterpretation.

The literal reading, then, with its acceptance of the essential accuracy of the narrator's reporting of events, seems to agree with the available evidence, both internal and external; while interpretations that assert the narrator's guilt cannot account for such an important detail of the story as the epigraph and are flatly contradicted by the author's own statement of his intention. Even if these interpretations were more convincing, however, they could be dismissed because they are unnecessary. "Ligeia" makes perfect sense when read literally, and Poe gives no clear

[6] Gargano, pp. 337–338.
[7] Muriel West, "Poe's 'Ligeia,' " *The Explicator*, XXII (October 1963), Item 15.
[8] Stovall, p. 421.

hint that it should be read otherwise. Perhaps an adaptation of the scientist's principle of parsimony would be helpful in settling such disputes as to what actually happens (as distinguished from symbolic or allegorical interpretations of those events) in a work of fiction. Of two hypothetical explanations of the same phenomena, assuming that both adequately account for every detail, the simpler one should be preferred *because* it is simpler.

Such a principle would not deny the complexity and range of meaning inherent in serious literature, but it would impose a useful humility on the critic, a recognition that interpretation must have its limits and that it is not his job to introduce gratuitous complications. Symbolic readings of "Ligeia" would remain possible, but to be valid they would have to be founded on the actual events of the tale. Thus Richard Wilbur's elaborate allegorizing in his essay on Poe in *Major Writers of America* is partly invalidated by his assumption that "the narrator is, in truth, the sole agent." Even when symbolic criticisms differ widely, it can reasonably be held that in some sense the tale contains or at least permits them, but this latitude does not extend to readings of the physical happenings. The principle of ambiguity does not apply in such cases. Either the narrator does or does not murder Rowena, either Ligeia revivifies in the body of Rowena and the apparent corpse rises from the death-bed, or the narrator has suffered a hallucination. The critic must choose, and in "Ligeia" there should be no great difficulty in making this choice.

Style and Meaning in "Ligeia"
and "William Wilson"

by Donald Barlow Stauffer

From his own lifetime to the present, controversy has flourished between those holding the widely accepted but inadequately demonstrated view that Poe was a master stylist and those who condemn his style for its awkwardness and lack of taste. Judgments upon his style, in fact, differ as widely as those making them, Hawthorne praising his "force and originality," Mark Twain finding his prose unreadable. Baudelaire's practically unrestrained praise of Poe's "admirable style, pure and bizarre" is balanced by the twentieth-century condemnation of Yvor Winters, who holds that Poe was always a bad writer, accidentally and temporarily popular.[1]

Many readers whose opinions lie somewhere between these extremes still often too hastily condemn Poe's style because they are using standards of "taste" or propriety which are seldom related to consideration of the style in the individual tales themselves. No judgment of the quality of a style can legitimately be made separately from a critical consideration of the work in which it is found. It is often disturbing to find remarks about the style of an author which seem to be based on the reader's own personal tastes, rather than upon his awareness that the style is inseparable from the work itself and must therefore, like its symbols, its metaphors, and its paradoxes, be organically related to it. Such an assumption must be insisted upon in the instance of Poe, who was not a careless, haphazard writer, but a conscious and skilled

---

"Style and Meaning in 'Ligeia' and 'William Wilson'" by Donald Barlow Stauffer. *From* Studies in Short Fiction II (*1965*), *pp. 316–18, 321–30. Copyright © 1965 by Newberry College. Reprinted by permission of* Studies in Short Fiction.

[1] [XVII, 232–233]; Mark Twain, letter to William Dean Howells, Jan. 18, 1909, in *Mark Twain-Howells Letters*, Henry Nash Smith and William M. Gibson, eds. (Cambridge, Mass., 1960), II, 841; Charles Baudelaire, "Edgar Poe: sa Vie et ses Oeuvres," introduction to *Histoires Extraordinaires par Edgar Poe* (Paris, 1856); and Yvor Winters, "Edgar Allan Poe: A Crisis in the History of American Obscurantism," *Maule's Curse* (Norfolk, Conn., 1938), p. 93.

craftsman—technician even—who carefully calculated the means by which to bring about his celebrated "unity of effect."

Allen Tate, who is more generous to Poe than many other modern critics, still has reservations about his style in some of his tales. Setting two passages together, one from "William Wilson" and one from "Ligeia," Tate concludes that he finds it difficult to admire what he calls the "ungrammatical rubbish" of the "Ligeia" passage. But, he says,

> . . . if Poe is worth understanding at all (I assume that he is), we might begin by asking why the writer of the lucid if not very distinguished passage from "William Wilson" repeatedly fell into the bathos of "Ligeia." I confess that Poe's serious style at its typical worst makes the reading of more than one story at a sitting an almost insuperable task.

Poe's subjects, he writes, are done up in a "glutinous prose" that "so fatigues one's attention that with the best will in the world one gives up, unless one gets a clue to the power underlying the flummery." [2]

There is the strong suggestion in these and other remarks by Tate that, stylistically, "William Wilson" and "Ligeia" are poles apart, and that the former, which is "perspicuous in diction and on the whole credible in realistic detail," is therefore to be preferred to the latter. But is the matter this simple? Closer inspection shows us that some of what looks very much like the "ungrammatical rubbish" of "Ligeia" can be found in "William Wilson." And much of "Ligeia," on the other hand, is written in a style not so different from that in many passages of "William Wilson." Actually, as I shall attempt to show, the same stylistic elements appear in both stories. The difference in the total effect produced by stylistic means derives from the difference in order and proportion of various stylistic ingredients rather than from the kind of polarity which Tate's remarks suggest. . . .

I

Looking first at "Ligeia," [3] we notice that the style is in many ways extravagant, lying somewhere between the youthful exuberance and heterogeneity of "The Assignation," and the ratiocinative and expository prose of "The Murders in the Rue Morgue." One of the first things we notice about the style of "Ligeia" is its incantatory quality, which makes us feel that the narrator is intoning his story. Rhythm and sound effects, especially in the opening paragraphs, are extremely im-

---

[2] Allen Tate, *The Forlorn Demon* (Chicago, 1933), p. 90.
[3] I have added references only for long quotations in this essay.—ED.

portant in establishing the tone of the tale. . . . Other stylistic traits
which occur to a noticeable extent . . . in "Ligeia" are repetition, inversions, and parenthetical expressions. Repetition, like the use of certain rhythmic patterns, gives his style an incantatory quality: "her wild
desire for life—for life—*but* for life." Ligeia's voice "grew more gentle
—grew more low." And emphasis is achieved by such expressions as
"far more, very far more" and "a too-too glorious effulgence." The
irrational quality of this kind of writing becomes even more evident
when we pull from context the phrases of which it is composed. Such is
the case also with inversions of normal word order, a device which
gives the style a distant, archaic, otherworldly tone: "In the classical
tongues was she deeply proficient." (Note the choice of *tongues* instead
of *languages*, and note also how different in tone is a more nearly nor-
mally ordered phrase: "In the classical languages she was deeply proficient," or "She was deeply proficient in the classical languages.")
Other inversions occur throughout the story: ". . . not until the last
instance . . . was shaken the external placidity of her demeanor";
". . . in death only was I fully impressed"; "For long hours . . .
would she pour out . . . the overflowing of a heart."

Poe consistently uses parenthetical expressions in "Ligeia" to emphasize or heighten the mood. Frequently they are in the form of interjec-
tions or exclamations: "a love, alas! all unmerited, all unworthily
bestowed"; "And (strange, oh, strangest mystery of all!)"; "I could re-
store her to the pathways she had abandoned—ah, *could* it be forever?
—upon the earth." All of these heighten the emotional tone, or in
some way emphasize the disturbed psychological state of the narrator.
Another smacks of Poe's particular brand of hokum, but it, too, is
consistent with the mood of the passage, "And there are one or two
stars in heaven (one especially, a star of the sixth magnitude, double
and changeable, to be found near the large star in Lyra) in a telescopic
scrutiny of which I have been made aware of the feeling."

The use of what W. M. Forrest, in a discussion of the biblical qualities of Poe's style,[4] has described as the "genitive of possession" is another syntactical feature giving an archaic or exotic texture to the style.
"The learning of Ligeia"; "the eyes of Ligeia"; "the person of Ligeia";
"the fetters of Death"; "the acquisition of Ligeia" are more frequent
than "Ligeia's eyes" or "Ligeia's beauty." The effect of this construction, and others in which *of* appears, such as "The hue of the orbs was
the most brilliant of black, and, far over them, hung jetty lashes of
great length," is, like the effect of inversion, repetition, and the use of

---

[4] William M. Forrest, *Biblical Allusions in Poe* (New York, 1928), p. 86.

exclamatory parentheses, a heightening, an emotionality, a sense of the mysterious, the irrational and the unreal.

Much, but by no means all, of "Ligeia" is written in this half-hysterical, highly emotional style, since Poe varies the style in this tale as he does in almost all his serious tales. Later in the tale we discover a much more measured, rational tone, as the narrator describes the fantastic interiors of the English abbey to which he retires after the death of Ligeia. The center portion is marked by complex, compound, and compound-complex sentences quite different from the simpler syntax of sentences in the early part of the tale. In his recollections of Ligeia he has been rhapsodic, conveying to the reader the frame of mind into which the memory of her puts him; now, in the second half of the tale, as he recalls the sequence of events leading up to the reappearance of Ligeia, he attempts to get a grip on himself and his emotions as he recounts the early history of Rowena dispassionately and with apparent detachment. He tries to view his actions and his taste for arabesque interiors with some objectivity—and even asks how the bride's family permitted her "to pass the threshold of an apartment *so* bedecked." But as he again recalls the evidence of his own senses, the narrator dwells on details of the appearance of the dying woman in a "naturalistic" description as he endeavors by this means to explain the inexplicable. He reports the "facts" as nearly as he can remember them. But as he draws nearer in memory to the appearance of Ligeia, he becomes more irrationally affected by that memory, and the last paragraph differs markedly in style from those preceding it. Inversions, repetitions, questions, exclamations, dashes, italics, capitals are all there, ending with the wild speech of the narrator himself with Poe's calculated use of repetition and parallelism for a maximum of emotional effect: "can I never—can I never be mistaken—these are the full, and the black, and the wild eyes—of my lost love—of the lady—of the LADY LIGEIA. . . ." [5]

But many passages in the [tale's] second half indicate quite clearly that Poe was in control of his material and knew what he was about in his treatment of it. Balanced sentence structure and a painstaking building-up of circumstantial detail surrounding the reappearance of Ligeia demonstrate that he was carefully and patiently combining—denying as usual the office of inspiration in the act of creation. The

[5] I am following the reading by James Schroeter in "A Misreading of Poe's 'Ligeia,'" *PMLA*, LXXVI (1961), 397–406, which examines and rejects many of the hypotheses made by Roy P. Basler in his well-known and influential essay "The Interpretation of 'Ligeia,'" *College English*, V (1944), 363–372 [Reprinted in *TCV*, pp. 51–63].

emotion of the narrator of "Ligeia" should not, of course, be confused
with the emotion of the author, and such obvious devices as the narrator's parenthetical "(what marvel that I shudder while I write?)"
should be read as part of Poe's deliberate effort to give the narrator's
emotions an air of verisimilitude. In dismissing the style of "Ligeia" as
ungrammatical rubbish, then, Tate most certainly exaggerates, for most
of it *is* grammatical and indeed much of it is highly ordered, highly
formal prose. The predominantly emotional quality of its style may be
defended by its appropriateness to both the agitated mental state of the
narrator and to the supernatural events he relates. . . .

II

Analysis of the style of "William Wilson" shows it to be a carefully
written story. Although it is interspersed with passages reminiscent of
the style of "Ligeia," it is dominated by the eighteenth-century *ordon-
nance* mentioned by Tate. The style, for the most part, is highly ordered, marked by connectives and transitional elements, balanced and
periodic sentences, a relatively high level of abstraction, little concrete
imagery (outside of the descriptions of the school of Wilson's boyhood),
few vivid adjectives, and a precision of diction. Certain key passages
deviate from this pattern, notably the first and last paragraphs.

In this tale Poe seems to be concentrating not on creating a poetic
effect but rather on telling a tale rationally and logically. Mood is
therefore secondary to the orderly development of a series of causally
related events. Certain qualities which were latent in the style of his
early tales, and which are more evident in his critical writing, are
highly developed and fully exploited here: parallelism; a measured
rhythm (the rhythm of good prose, not "rhythmic prose," as in "Ligeia"); and abstract diction, which is sometimes latinate, sometimes
cumbersome and even ludicrous. This diction combines with the order-
liness of his sentence structure to give his prose a particularly eighteenth-century quality. The pace of the story, which is dictated by the
formal style resulting from longer sentences, is leisurely but not halting, measured rather than uneven. . . .

The dominant stylistic note of the tale is not struck until the third
paragraph, in which the narrator begins to relate the sequence of
events in a dispassionate, rational, analytical style. Analysis is the key-
note of Wilson's remarks; in fact, we may say that Poe wrote "William
Wilson" in the language of *analysis,* as contrasted to the language of
emotion in which he wrote most of "Ligeia." The narrator of "William
Wilson" constantly subjects himself and the motives for his actions to a

careful scrutiny, evidently in an effort to answer the questions he has
so passionately posed in the opening paragraph. The narrative intention of this scrutiny is clear enough. Wilson, at a loss to account satis-
factorily for the state of spiritual death and moral depravity in which
he finds himself at the opening of the tale, attempts to exercise his
faculties of reason and analysis over the sequence of events which led
to its disastrous conclusion. He therefore begins by carefully noting his
inherited characteristics: he is descended from a race of "imaginative
and easily excitable temperament"—and he develops into a child who
is "self-willed, addicted to the wildest caprices, and a prey to the most
ungovernable passions." Driven by his impulse to recall and analyze
his extraordinary behavior, Wilson then turns to "minute recollections"
of his first school days. Like Egæus in "Berenice," he seeks relief in
"the weakness of a few rambling details." But he also attributes meaning to these details: ". . . the first ambiguous monitions of the destiny
which afterward so fully overshadowed me." These school-day recollections take up fully a third of the story, recollections which he finds
"stamped upon memory in lines as vivid, as deep, and as durable as the
exergues of the Carthaginian medals." Most of them relate to the character of the schoolmate with the remarkable resemblance to himself.
Only a great many quotations would demonstrate the analytic quality
of the style of this section of the tale, the number of times which Wilson speculates on the possible causes for having understood or misun-
derstood the conduct of his double, and the descriptions of his relationship with him. I shall quote two:

> I could only conceive this singular behavior to arise from a consummate
> self-conceit assuming the vulgar airs of patronage and protection.
> Perhaps it was this latter trait in Wilson's conduct, conjoined with our
> identity of name, and the mere accident of our having entered the school
> upon the same day, which set afloat the notion that we were brothers,
> among the senior classes in the academy. [III, 306]

> Wilson's retaliations in kind were many; and there was one form of
> his practical wit that disturbed me beyond measure. How his sagacity first
> discovered at all that so petty a thing would vex me, is a question I never
> could solve; but having discovered, he habitually practised the annoyance.
> I had always felt aversion to my uncourtly patronymic, and its very com-
> mon, if not plebian praenomen. [III, 308]

Both of these passages are typical of the dominant style of the tale:
highly abstract, rather stilted—even mannered. Because it is not heavily
latinate, the latinate expressions themselves seem actually to be affecta-
tions: *sagacity, consummate*; and sometimes even absurd: *patronymic,
plebeian praenomen*. These words give a weightiness to certain sen-

tences which the subject hardly demands. But more to the immediate
point is the language of speculation and conjecture: *perhaps, conceive,
solve.* These words suggest that the narrator is constantly attempting to
analyze and explain rationally the motives for his actions; something
which the narrator of "Ligeia" does not do.

Formality and order, then, are the chief characteristics of the dominant style of "William Wilson," and parallelism is one of the syntactical devices through which Poe achieves these. Note, for example, the
eighteenth-century quality of this passage: ". . . a profligacy which
set at defiance the laws, while it eluded the vigilance of the institution."
Or this: "He appeared to be destitute alike of the ambition which
urged, and of the passionate energy of mind which enabled me to ex-
cel." These parallelisms are different in their logical clarity from the
predominantly emotional quality of similar constructions in "Ligeia."

Formality of sentence structure is achieved in other ways as well. In
this sentence are three successive phrases, each composed of three elements, and in the final coupling of two phrases modifying *affectionateness,* each phrase contains three modifiers:

> In his rivalry he might have been supposed actuated solely by a whimsical
> desire to thwart, astonish, or mortify myself; although there were times
> when I could not help observing, with a feeling made of wonder, abase-
> ment, and pique, that he mingled with his injuries, his insults, or his con-
> tradictions, a certain most inappropriate, and assuredly most unwelcome
> *affectionateness* of manner. [III, 306]

Such formal groupings of three elements are often found in Poe's
periodic sentences (periods also occur more frequently in "William
Wilson" than they do in "Ligeia"): "That the school, indeed, did not
feel his design, perceive its accomplishment, and participate in his
sneer. . . ." Less formal groupings of threes occur not only in the
formal rational style, but also in Poe's emotional style, as in the first
paragraph of "William Wilson," suggesting, therefore, that such groupings are a characteristic trait of all of Poe's styles.

But the stylistic trait which at the same time links these two tales and
indicates their essential difference is the parenthetical expression.
"Ligeia," we have observed, is full of parentheses. "William Wilson"
has many, if not more. But while in the former they are used to
heighten or emphasize the mood or atmosphere by their exclamatory or
interjectional character, in this tale they slow down the pace by quali-
fying and amplifying ideas. The parentheses in "William Wilson" are
halting, hesitant, fussy, over-precise, reflecting the deliberations of a
mind committed to discovering the truth. They contain additional,
sometimes gratuitous, information that seems to satisfy the narrator's

overwhelming need for facts and details. They also reflect the complexity of his mind, a complexity already more than once suggested by the references to the "many little nooks and recesses" of which the school mansion is composed. If the tale is symbolically a mental journey, this "wilderness of narrow passages" suggests the labyrinthine quality of the mind itself. Thus the style, which is itself full of similar nooks and recesses, becomes organically related to Wilson's own psychological state. The following passage illustrates the kinds of parentheses (indicated by brackets)—and parentheses within parentheses—typical of the style of "William Wilson":

> . . . but, [in the latter months of my residence at the academy,] [although the intrusion of his ordinary manner had,] [beyond doubt,] [in some measure, abated,] my sentiments, [in nearly similar proportion,] partook very much of positive hatred. Upon one occasion he saw this, [I think;] and afterward avoided, [or made a show of avoiding] me.
>
> It was about the same period, [if I remember aright,] that, [in an altercation of violence with him,] [in which he was more than usually thrown off his guard, and spoke and acted with an openness of demeanor rather foreign to his nature,] I discovered, [or fancied I discovered,] in his accent, in his air, and general appearance, a something which first startled, and then deeply interested me, by bringing to mind dim visions of my earliest infancy—wild, confused and thronging memories of a time when memory herself was yet unborn. [III, 310–11]

The general character and function of these parentheses in "William Wilson," then, differ radically from those of the intensifying parentheses of "Ligeia." Here they are authorial comments written not in an emotional frenzy but in the coolness of recollection. They often have not only an analytic but a strongly moralistic tone as well. For example: "It was no doubt the anomalous state of affairs existing between us, which turned all my attacks upon him (and there were many, either open or covert) into the channel of banter or practical joke (giving pain while assuming the aspect of mere fun). . . ." Or even more overtly moral in tone: "I was anxiously seeking (let me not say with what unworthy motive) the young, the gay, the beautiful wife of the aged and doting Di Broglio." Syntax in this tale, then, is actually a means of characterization, since the narrator's use of parentheses gives the impression of a man extremely interested in being both accurate and honest. . . .

At first reading, "Ligeia" and "William Wilson" seem entirely dissimilar in style, yet the more closely we examine them, the more similarities we find. The reason for these similarities—as well as the differences—lies partly in the similarity of structure and theme. In "Ligeia" the narrator is attempting to reproduce the state of mind he was in when he was in contact with Ligeia. This state of mind is evoked in the beginning and vanishes with the death of Ligeia. With the narrator's move to England and the return of his rational faculties, the style resembles the rational style of "William Wilson." But as the symptoms of Rowena's disease become more and more evident, the narrator gradually discards the rational style, in which he has attempted clinically to recall every detail of the circumstances of Ligeia's return, and returns to the state of mind he was in on that memorable night. His final outburst recalls the style, and even echoes some of the words, of the opening passages of the tale, thereby relating the beginning of the tale to the end. The mood and attitude of the speaker are primarily nostalgic, or evocative, as he attempts to reproduce in his own mind, as well as in the mind of the reader, an idea of what he experienced. This attempt to relate the barely perceived world, of which only the poet may achieve momentary glimpses, to the things of this world which bear only an imperfect relation to them, is the attempt Poe makes in all his poetry. But language fails him, as he himself is aware, and only by calling up an atmosphere roughly analogous to what he has perceived can the narrator-hero-poet hope to put what is untranslatable into words.

We may similarly read "William Wilson" as a parable of the war between the external world and the world of the spirit. Whereas in "Ligeia" the hero has renounced the physical world and achieved a momentary union with the absolute, in this tale Wilson has succumbed to the corrupting material world and has thereby lost his soul. Both tales begin in recollection and end in hysteria, but "William Wilson" is not so much an attempt to reproduce the quality of his experience, which he finds almost unendurably painful, as an attempt to trace the *causes* leading up to it. The experience itself, therefore, although it comes at a climactic moment in both tales, is not as important in "William Wilson" as are the causally related events leading up to it. One indication of the difference in emphasis in the two tales is that in "Ligeia" we know from the outset that she is dead, but we do not learn of the death of Wilson's double until the end; we know only that Wilson has committed an "unpardonable crime." The direction of "William Wilson" is towards rediscovery—not of the moment of confrontation, which nevertheless is inevitable, but of the sequence of events leading up to it. In short, the narrator of "William Wilson" finds himself in a fallen state and seeks a rational explanation for it; the narrator of "Ligeia" finds himself in a state of lost happiness and seeks to reproduce that happiness—hence the difference in stylistic organization and emphasis.

"The Black Cat": Perverseness Reconsidered

by James W. Gargano

The temptation to accept the events in Edgar Allan Poe's "The Black Cat" as inexplicable is enforced by the narrator's repeated assertion that he cannot understand his own story. Moreover, when he volunteers "explanations," he assigns as the "cause" of his deeds the motiveless spirit of perverseness, a radical "impulse of the human heart" to act irrationally. If the narrator is to be taken at his word, his hanging of the black cat and his final self-betrayal to the police can be conveniently regarded as manifestations of the soul's perverse desire "to offer violence to its own nature" [V, 146]. Since the reader cannot analyze this irreducible, elemental perverseness, "The Black Cat" may be accepted as advocating the thesis that the causes of human conduct defy intellectual scrutiny. Moreover, to grant Poe's protagonist his belief in an uncontrollable and enigmatic imp of the perverse is, perforce, to agree with him in explaining away, as naïve and illogical, any moral rationale of life; for as an erratic plaything of an inscrutable force, man cannot accept the notion of personal responsibility or of a system of explicable values to which his conduct must conform.

Yet, certain comments by the narrator imply that his behavior can perhaps be reduced to ordinary psychological and moral laws. First of all, he admits the possibility that "some intellect more calm, more logical and far less excitable than my own . . . will perceive, in the circumstances I detail with awe, nothing more than an ordinary succession of very natural causes and effects" [V, 143]. Secondly, in describing the fire that followed his hanging of the cat, he incites his reader to search for logical and moral relations between the two events by refusing all too glibly "to establish a sequence of cause and effect between the disaster and the atrocity" [V, 147]. In addition to the narrator's comments, the arrangement of incidents in the tale suggests "develop-

" 'The Black Cat': Perverseness Reconsidered" by James W. Gargano. From Texas Studies in Language and Literature II (1960), pp. 172-8. Copyright © 1960 by the University of Texas Press, Austin. Reprinted by permission of the University of Texas Press.

ment" rather than accident. Next to his own statement that he is a victim of the imp of the perverse, we must place the evidence of a gradual enfeebling of his moral nature under the impact of increasing self-indulgence. Finally, his frenetic deeds and rationalizations have all the appearance of a blind attempt to escape from ineluctable moral consequences whose authority he unconsciously admits by contemptuous derogations of them. He resembles William Wilson in his schizophrenia, but he is more subtly intellectual than Wilson in fabricating an ingenious dialectic to explain his moral aberrations.

Far from being a mere treatise on perverseness, "The Black Cat" is on one level an intense study of the protagonist's discovery of, and infatuated immersion in, evil, and on another level a subtle examination of the protagonist's refusal to recognize the moral meaning of his career. To demonstrate how these themes can be found in the story, however, it is necessary to recognize Poe's essentially symbolic approach to his material. For, taken literally, the details of the story would be embarrassing even to the most shameless animal lover; it is an outrageous excess that the narrator should, for the hanging of a cat, condemn himself as having committed "a deadly sin that would so jeopardize my immortal soul as to place it—if such a thing were possible—even beyond the reach of the infinite mercy of the Most Merciful and Most Terrible God" [V, 147]. That a fire should be almost mystically visited upon the house of an executioner of a cat is also absurd. Finally, the manner in which the vengeful cat exposes the over-confident criminal at the end of the story is improbable even for a Gothic melodrama. If read unimaginatively, then, "The Black Cat" is so mystifying that the narrator seems for once reasonable when declaring that he can "neither expect nor solicit belief" in it [V, 143].

Analysis of "The Black Cat" may profitably begin with a consideration of the narrator's professed tenderness of heart. This distinguishing trait expresses itself in such an inordinate fondness for animals as to call forth the ridicule of his playmates. Obviously his sentimental excesses, his extreme happiness in feeding and caressing his pets, characterize him as deriving his sharpest pleasures from a sensationalism which suggests an unhealthy overdevelopment of the voluptuary side of his nature. He lives snugly and self-delusively in a world of private gratifications, making his intimacy with his pets a substitute for "the paltry friendship and gossamer fidelity of mere *Man*" [V, 144]. His marriage introduces little change into his life, for his wife shares his docility and tenderness. Indeed, it is almost as if he has acquired another pet rather than a spouse. This congenial triumvirate—narrator, wife, and pets, especially Pluto, the black cat—appears for a time to constitute a family from which all but soft and gentle sensations have been eliminated.

The narrator's private world, however, cannot endure unchallenged because, as he does not see, it is essentially unwholesome in affording expression to only one side of his nature. In spite of his fantasy of establishing the reign of tenderness in his household, his own mixed self dictates the mixed nature of reality. What the narrator fails to perceive is that his single-minded affectionateness is itself an abnormality, for it thrives on a wanton ignorance of his own ambivalence. Instead, then, of being an indication of innate goodness, his exaggerated devotion to his wife and Pluto is a symptom of an unstable sensibility. Moreover, his failure to understand his effusive tenderness provides the first intimation of his persistent inability to explain his acts and motives.

The end of the "friendship" is brought about by the narrator's lapse into intemperance. Although his tirade against "alcohol" fixes a specific cause for this change of character, his helplessness under the power of "the Fiend Intemperance" symbolizes his susceptibility to evil through his own divided nature. He has discovered a side of himself which encroaches upon and soon seeks to engulf all other facets of the self. Now, in abusing his wife with "intemperate language" and "personal violence" and in mistreating his pets, he not only destroys his "happy" ménage but begins to project his own altered vision into things outside himself. In other words, the world, becoming fractured into good and evil, will turn against him to the extent that he turns against himself. Having re-created reality in accordance with his own vision, he fancies that "the cat avoided my presence" [V, 145]. Pluto, who had been his favorite, now possesses a special malevolence and becomes the witch the narrator's wife had humorously called him.

In the beginning of the story, the black cat is unmistakably neutral, neither good nor bad. Apparently, however, it changes its role with every psychological alteration in its owner: it is at first merely docile, like the narrator and his wife; later as the narrator resorts to violence, it naturally bites him; it then becomes an innocent victim; and finally it returns, in a reincarnation, to betray the now complacent murderer of his wife. The cat, then, must be understood not realistically but symbolically. It is the narrator's own multiple nature, its mild disposition momentarily distracting attention from its suggestive blackness and its name implying that for all its tender responsiveness it has potentially infernal qualities. To put it briefly, once the total self is outraged, the subterranean king, Pluto, tyrannically exacts his vengeance.

In such terms, the narrator's "fiendish malevolence" in cutting Pluto's eye out from its socket can be easily related to the theme of the story. The mutilation represents the narrator's compulsive assault upon himself and a partial obliteration of his vision of good. Well might he declare that his "original soul seemed, at once, to take flight from my body." In referring to the atrocity as "damnable," he is not, on the symbolic level on which the tale must be read, indulging in hyperbole; for he has committed a "crime" whose effect can be seen in the deadening of his moral sense:

> I experienced a sentiment half of horror, half of remorse, for the crime of which I had been guilty; but it was, at best, a feeble and equivocal feeling, and the soul remained untouched [V, 145–46].

His obduracy and lack of insight are further evident in the new excuses which cause him to lose all remembrance of his evil. Permanently maimed, he is now ready to violate himself in a more complete manner.

Before describing the hanging of Pluto, the narrator disregards his earlier decision "to place before the world, plainly, succinctly, and *without comment*, a series of mere household events" [V, 143; my italics]. Instead, he presents a short disquisition on the "spirit of Perverseness," which he defines as "one of the indivisible primary faculties or sentiments, which give direction to the character of man." It is characteristic of this spirit, willfully and with the actor's apparent knowledge of the ensuing evil, to act in direct opposition to Law. It compels man to choose, irrationally, to do the precise deed that will cause him to affront and injure himself; it is "an unfathomable longing of the soul *to vex itself*—to offer violence to its own nature—to do wrong for the wrong's sake only" [V, 146].

Exonerating himself of responsibility for his outrage, the narrator invokes this spirit of perverseness to explain his hanging of Pluto: weeping and remorseful, he murders the cat in "cold blood" and, with horror and shame for the sin he commits, he alienates himself from the mercy of God. Yet, in spite of the narrator's insistence that perverseness is an uncaused cause, "one of the indivisible primary faculties," his transgression is not without relation to his earlier misdeeds. In fact, it appears as a climax to them, for unable to endure the reproach implicit in the disfigured, half-blind symbol of his former docility and kindness, he must exterminate it and thus emancipate himself from it. The narrator's rational attempt to explain away his responsibility seems to me a result of his atrophied moral sense. As will be shown, he continually rejects obvious moral explanations in favor of either spurious and ingenious rationalizations or admissions of his inability to determine the cause-and-effect relationship between the events of his life.

Immediately after the destruction of Pluto, the narrator demonstrates incorrigible moral obtuseness by failing to understand the significance of the fire that consumes all but one wall of his house. Certainly, the first must be seen as punishment for the "crime," but it is also the symbolic end of the first phase of the narrator's life. The destruction of the house clearly represents his almost complete moral disintegration, as in "The Fall of the House of Usher" the collapse of the fissure-ridden house corresponds to the death of Roderick Usher. The remaining wall with the "portraiture" of Pluto on it just as clearly signifies that what survives of the narrator will be haunted by his ineradicable sin against his own nature. Yet, in his account of the fire, he disdains "the weakness of seeking to establish a sequence of cause and effect, between the disaster and the atrocity." Moreover, when his neighbors gape at the firm impression of the cat's body in the wall, he proceeds to elaborate a theory which "readily accounted to my reason, if not altogether to my conscience, for the startling fact" [V, 148]. Obviously then, the narrator's version of the "mere household events" cannot be accepted uncritically, nor, I believe, can his self-exculpating theory of perverseness. He is, of course, eager to introduce into a world of psychological and moral order a concept that eliminates the onus of responsibility and guilt. Indeed, one of the most telling points of "The Black Cat" is the narrator's fatuous denial of a moral order at the same time that the reader observes its unfaltering operation. This dramatic irony seems to me one of the compelling artistic effects that make "The Black Cat" an undisputed masterpiece. Most critics, I feel, underestimate the sophistication and power of the story by accepting the narrator's apologetics as representing Poe's version of reality. This error, I am convinced, stems from the widespread critical assumption that, since Poe's tales are largely autobiographical, the narrator and author can be regarded as one and the same.

Some observations on the story's structure are in order at this point. First of all, the incidents from the beginning of the story up to and including the fire constitute a distinct artistic unit: a climactic deed has been consummated and a radical moral change has taken place in the protagonist. In a sense, the first section establishes, metaphorically, the conditions that must precede the narrator's murder of his wife. The artistry of the section is remarkable, for in addition to dramatizing what appears a "complete" action, it leaves the protagonist on the brink of total self-destruction.

If there was any doubt of the narrator's evasive and inadequate interpretations of his degeneration, the second section, resembling the relentless unfolding of inevitable consequences, clarifies Poe's total intention. Though the incidents somewhat parallel those of the first section, the intensity suggests that the issues are to be even more permanently resolved. The return of Pluto's counterpart enforces the message of the portraiture on the enduring wall; the hanged cat, now the grim prophet of doom, bears on its breast a white "splotch," which distinctly shapes itself into a "GALLOWS" [V,149,151]. Clearly, Pluto's fate intimates that the actual fate of the narrator has, morally speaking, been already decided. Having in a furtive manner mutilated himself and thus cut himself off from the resources and nourishment of his moral nature, he must more publicly proclaim his own evil. Strictly, the conflagration has demonstrated his guilt and the image of Pluto on the wall has exposed him to his neighbors. But what is secretly perpetrated in the first section, must, in the second section, be revealed openly to society. The hanging of the cat is the clandestine equivalent to the humanly revolting murder of his wife; they are the same deed, in the latter case taking a form which outrages society and must be punished by it. The exposés, too, are very similar: in the first instance the cat's image in the wall convicts the narrator of sin as surely as in the second instance the corpse of his murdered wife does, but in the second instance the "spectators" have no doubt about the heinousness of the offense. Thus, the two parts of "The Black Cat" effectively complement each other by revealing in turn the narrator's inner deterioration and his public exposure.

In the second part of the story, it must be added, the protagonist continues to ignore the moral nature of life just as stubbornly as he did in propounding the theory of perverseness; foolishly, he concludes that in killing and disposing of his wife (whose death heralds the disappearance of the second cat) he has permanently rid himself of guilt and moral considerations. His life, he believes, has been simplified because he no longer feels divided; he takes intellectual comfort in the supposition that he has demonstrated his superiority to moral order:

> The second and the third day passed, and still my tormentor (the cat) came not. Once again I breathed as a freeman. The monster in terror had fled the premises forever! I should behold it no more! My happiness was supreme! The guilt of my dark deed disturbed me but little. . . . I looked upon my future felicity as secured. [V, 154]

His rationalizations, however, do not (as the perverseness rationalization did not) square with the facts, for the "cat" is concealed in the depths of a nature still perversely divided and he is, in spite of his protestations to the contrary, highly disturbed. His swaggering confidence in the presence of the police represents, I feel, a blind trust in the power of his intellect to triumph over the superstitions which he feels are formulated in the moral code. (It will be remembered that in the first section of the story he once dismissed his wife's "superstitions" about black cats.) Yet, ironically, his frantic invitations to the police to examine the house with care attest to the subtle influence of Pluto in his role of avenger. When most assured, the narrator is really weakest; for his house, like the intellectual fabrications through which he desires to escape his conscience, is not so well constructed as he persists in describing it.

Again the house must be interpreted symbolically, for once again the "collusion" of cat and house exposes his guilt:

> "Bye the bye, gentlemen, this—this is a very well constructed house."
> [In the rabid desire to say something easily, I scarcely knew what I uttered at all.]—"I may say an *excellently* constructed house. These walls—are you going, gentlemen?—These walls are solidly put together." [V, 155]

But with the final wail of the cat (unmistakably his walled-up wife, cat, and conscience), he swoons with the knowledge that his new house is as flimsy as the one consumed by fire.

Finally, however, the illumination or insight that his catastrophe should force upon the narrator never comes. Perversely convinced that what has happened to him lacks cause and effect, he betrays almost complete moral insensitivity even as he is about to be executed by the agents of the very Law he has flouted and attempted to explain away. To accept his specious intellectual dodges as the point of "The Black Cat," as so many critics do, is to exalt the very thing Poe is deriding in the narrator. If any perverseness exists in the story, it is the protagonist's perverseness in being able to dismiss a transparently moral adventure as a mere sequence of inexplicable events.

Poe's "The Tell-Tale Heart"

by E. Arthur Robinson

Poe's "The Tell-Tale Heart" consists of a monologue in which an accused murderer protests his sanity rather than his innocence. The point of view is the criminal's, but the tone is ironic in that his protestation of sanity produces an opposite effect upon the reader. From these two premises stem multiple levels of action in the story. The criminal, for example, appears obsessed with defending his psychic self at whatever cost, but actually his drive is self-destructive since successful defense upon either implied charge—of murder or of criminal insanity—automatically involves admission of guilt upon the other.

Specifically, the narrator bases his plea upon the assumption that madness is incompatible with systematic action, and as evidence of his capacity for the latter he relates how he has executed a horrible crime with rational precision. He reiterates this argument until it falls into a pattern: "If still you think me mad, you will think so no longer when I describe the wise precautions I took for concealment of the body" [V, 92]. At the same time he discloses a deep psychological confusion. Almost casually he admits lack of normal motivation: "Object there was none. Passion there was none. I loved the old man." Yet in spite of this affection he says that the idea of murder "haunted me day and night" [V, 88]. Since such processes of reasoning tend to convict the speaker of madness, it does not seem out of keeping that he is driven to confession by "hearing" reverberations of the still-beating heart in the corpse he has dismembered, nor that he appears unaware of the irrationalities in his defense of rationality.

At first reading, the elements of "The Tell-Tale Heart" appear simple: the story itself is one of Poe's shortest; it contains only two main characters, both unnamed, and three indistinguishable police officers; even the setting of the narration is left unspecified. In the present

"Poe's 'The Tell-Tale Heart'" by E. Arthur Robinson. From Nineteenth-Century Fiction XIX (1963), pp. 369–78. Copyright © 1963 by The Regents of the University of California. Reprinted by permission of Nineteenth-Century Fiction and E. Arthur Robinson.

study my object is to show that beneath its narrative flow the story illustrates the elaboration of design which Poe customarily sought, and also that it contains two of the major psychological themes dramatized in his longer works.

It is important to note that Poe's theory of art emphasizes development almost equally with unity of effect. There must be, he insists, "a repetition of purpose," a "dropping of the water upon the rock" [XI, 107]; thus he calls heavily upon the artist's craftsmanship to devise thematic modifications of the "preconceived effect." A favorite image in his stories is that of arabesque ornamentation with repetitive design. In "The Tell-Tale Heart" one can distinguish several such recurring devices filling out the "design" of the tale, the most evident being what the narrator calls his "over acuteness of the senses." He incorporates this physical keenness into his plea of sanity: ". . . why *will* you say that I am mad? The disease had sharpened my senses—not destroyed, not dulled them. Above all was the sense of hearing acute" [V, 88]. He likens the sound of the old man's heart to the ticking of a watch "enveloped in cotton" and then fancies that its terrified beating may arouse the neighbors [V, 91–92]. His sensitivity to sight is equally disturbing, for it is the old man's eye, "a pale blue eye, with a film over it" [V, 88], which first vexed him and which he seeks to destroy. Similar though less extreme powers are ascribed to the old man. For example, the murderer congratulates himself that not even his victim could have detected anything wrong with the floor which has been replaced over the body, and earlier he imagines the old man, awakened by "the first slight noise," listening to determine whether the sound has come from an intruder or "the wind in the chimney" [V, 90]. Variations such as these give the sensory details a thematic significance similar to that of the "morbid acuteness of the senses" of Roderick Usher in "The Fall of the House of Usher" or the intensity with which the victim of the Inquisition hears, sees, and smells his approaching doom in "The Pit and the Pendulum."

These sensory data provide the foundation for an interesting psychological phenomenon in the story. As the characters listen in the darkness, intervals of strained attention are prolonged until the effect resembles that of slow motion. Thus for seven nights the madman enters the room so "very, very slowly" that it takes him an hour to get his head through the doorway; as he says, "a watch's minute-hand moves more quickly than did mine." When on the eighth night the old man is alarmed, "for a whole hour I did not move a muscle" [V, 89–90]. Later he is roused to fury by the man's terror, but "even yet," he declares, "I refrained and kept still. I scarcely breathed" [V, 91]. On different nights both men sit paralyzed in bed, listening for terrors real or imagined. After the murder is completed, "I placed my hand upon the heart and held it there many minutes" [V, 92]. In the end it seems to his overstrained nerves that the police officers linger inordinately in the house, chatting and smiling, until he is driven frantic by their cheerful persistence.

This psychological process is important to "The Tell-Tale Heart" in two ways. First, reduplication of the device gives the story structural power. Poe here repeats a dominating impression at least seven times in a brief story. Several of the instances mentioned pertain to plot, but others function to emphasize the former and to provide aesthetic satisfaction. To use Poe's words, "by such means, with such care and skill, a picture is at length painted which leaves in the mind of him who contemplates it with a kindred art, a sense of the fullest satisfaction. The idea of the tale, its thesis, has been presented unblemished . . ." [XI, 108]. Here Poe is speaking specifically of "skilfully-constructed tales," and the complementary aspects of technique described are first to omit extraneous material and second to combine incidents, tone, and style to develop the "pre-established design." In this manner, form and "idea" become one. The thematic repetition and variation of incident in "The Tell-Tale Heart" offer one of the clearest examples of this architectural principle of Poe's at work.

Second, this slow-motion technique intensifies the subjectivity of "The Tell-Tale Heart" beyond that attained by mere use of a narrator. In the psychological triad of stimulus, internal response, and action, the first and third elements are slighted and the middle stage is given exaggerated attention.[1] In "The Tell-Tale Heart," stimulus in an objective sense scarcely exists at all. Only the man's eye motivates the murderer, and that almost wholly through his internal reaction to it. The action too, though decisive, is quickly over: "In an instant I dragged him to the floor, and pulled the heavy bed over him" [V, 92]. In contrast, the intermediate, subjective experience is prolonged to a point where psychologically it is beyond objective measurement. At first the intervals receive conventional description—an "hour," or "many minutes"—but eventually such designations become meaningless and duration can be presented only in terms of the experience

---

[1] Joseph Warren Beach in *The Twentieth-Century Novel* (New York, 1932), p. 407, describes a similar effect in stream-of-consciousness writing: "The subjective element becomes noticeable in fiction, as in everyday psychology, when an interval occurs between the stimulus to action and the resulting act." In extreme application of this technique, he declares, "there is a tendency to exhaust the content of the moment presented, there is *an infinite expansion of the moment*," and he adds that the danger is that "there may come to pass a disintegration of the psychological complex, a divorce between motive and conduct" (p. 409). This is close to the state of Poe's narrator and murderer.

itself. Thus, in the conclusion of the story, the ringing in the madman's ears first is "fancied," then later becomes "distinct," then is discovered to be so "definite" that it is erroneously accorded external actuality, and finally grows to such obsessive proportions that it drives the criminal into an emotional and physical frenzy. Of the objective duration of these stages no information is given; the experience simply "continued" until "at length" the narrator "found" that its quality had changed [V, 93–94].

Through such psychological handling of time Poe achieves in several of his most effective stories, including "The Tell-Tale Heart," two levels of chronological development which are at work simultaneously throughout the story. Typically, the action reaches its most intense point when the relation between the objective and subjective time sense falters or fails. At this point too the mental world of the subject is at its greatest danger of collapse. Thus we have the mental agony of the bound prisoner who loses all count of time as he alternately swoons and lives intensified existence while he observes the slowly descending pendulum. The narrator in "The Pit and the Pendulum" specifically refuses to accept responsibility for objective time-correlations: "There was another interval of utter insensibility; it was brief; for, upon again lapsing into life, there had been no perceptible descent in the pendulum. But it might have been long; for I knew there were demons who took note of my swoon, and who could have arrested the vibration at pleasure" [V, 79]. These demons are his Inquisitional persecutors, but more subjective "demons" are at work in the timeless terror and fascination of the mariner whirled around the abyss in "The Descent into the Maelström," or the powerless waiting of Usher for days after he first hears his sister stirring within the tomb. In each instance the objective world has been reduced to the microcosm of an individual's experience; his time sense fades under the pressure of emotional stress and physical paralysis.

Even when not literally present, paralysis often may be regarded as symbolic in Poe's stories. In *The Narrative of Arthur Gordon Pym* (1838), Pym's terrifying dreams in the hold of the ship represent physical and mental paralysis: "Had a thousand lives hung upon the movement of a limb or the utterance of a syllable, I could have neither stirred nor spoken. . . . I felt that my powers of body and mind were fast leaving me" [III, 28–29]. Other examples are the "convolutions" of bonds about the narrator in "The Pit and the Pendulum," the death-grasp on the ring-bolt in "The Descent into the Maelström," the inaction of Roderick and (more literally) the catalepsy of Madeline Usher, and in part the supposed rationality of the madman in "The Tell-Tale Heart," which turns out to be subservience of his mental to his emotional nature. In most applications of the slow-motion technique in "The Tell-Tale Heart," three states of being are present concurrently: emotional tension, loss of mental grasp upon the actualities of the situation, and inability to act or to act deliberately. Often these conditions both invite and postpone catastrophe, with the effect of focusing attention upon the intervening experience.

In the two years following publication of "The Tell-Tale Heart," Poe extended this timeless paralysis to fantasies of hypnosis lasting beyond death. "Mesmeric Revelation" (1844) contains speculations about the relation between sensory experience and eternity. In "The Facts in the Case of M. Valdemar" (1845) the hypnotized subject is maintained for nearly seven months in a state of suspended "death" and undergoes instant dissolution when revived. His pleading for either life or death suggests that his internal condition had included awareness and suffering. Similarly the narrator in "The Tell-Tale Heart" records: "Oh God! what *could* I do? I foamed—I raved—I swore!"—while all the time the police officers notice no foaming nor raving, for still they "chatted pleasantly, and smiled" [V, 94]. His reaction is still essentially subjective, although he paces the room and grates his chair upon the boards above the beating heart. All these experiences move toward ultimate collapse, which is reached in "The Tell-Tale Heart" as it is for Usher and the hypnotized victims, while a last-moment reprieve is granted in "The Pit and the Pendulum" and "The Descent into the Maelström."

A second major theme in "The Tell-Tale Heart" is the murderer's psychological identification with the man he kills. Similar sensory details connect the two men. The vulture eye which the subject casts upon the narrator is duplicated in the "single thin ray" [V, 89] of the lantern that falls upon his own eye; like the unshuttered lantern, it is always one eye that is mentioned, never two. One man hears the creaking of the lantern hinge, the other the slipping of a finger upon the fastening. Both lie awake at midnight "hearkening to the death-watches in the wall" [V, 90]. The loud yell of the murderer is echoed in the old man's shriek, which the narrator, as though with increasing clairvoyance, later tells the police was his own. Most of all the identity is implied in the key psychological occurrence in the story—the madman's mistaking his own heartbeat for that of his victim, both before and after the murder.

These two psychological themes—the indefinite extension of subjective time and the psychic merging of killer and killed—are linked closely together in the story. This is illustrated in the narrator's commentary after he has awakened the old man by an incautious sound and each waits for the other to move:

Presently I heard a slight groan, and I knew it was the groan of mortal terror. It was not a groan of pain or of grief—oh, no!—it was the low stifled sound that arises from the bottom of the soul when overcharged with awe. I knew the sound well. Many a night, just at midnight, when all the world slept, it has welled up from my own bosom, deepening, with its dreadful echo, the terrors that distracted me. I say I knew it well . . . I knew that he had been lying awake ever since the first slight noise, when he had turned in the bed. His fears had been ever since growing upon him. He had been trying to fancy them causeless, but could not. He had been saying to himself—"It is nothing but the wind in the chimney—it is only a mouse crossing the floor," or "it is merely a cricket which has made a single chirp." Yes, he had been trying to comfort himself with these suppositions: but he had found all in vain. [V, 90–91]

Here the slow-motion technique is applied to both characters, with emphasis upon first their subjective experience and second the essential identity of that experience. The madman feels compelled to delay the murder until his subject is overcome by the same nameless fears that have possessed his own soul. The groan is an "echo" of these terrors within. The speaker has attempted a kind of catharsis by forcing his own inner horror to arise in his companion and then feeding his self-pity upon it. This pity cannot prevent the murder, which is a further attempt at exorcism. The final two sentences of the paragraph quoted explain why he believes that destruction is inevitable:

All in vain; because Death, in approaching him, had stalked with his black shadow before him, and enveloped the victim. And it was the mournful influence of the unperceived shadow that caused him to feel —although he neither saw nor heard—to *feel* the presence of my head within the room. [V, 91]

The significance of these sentences becomes clearer when we consider how strikingly the over-all effect of time-extension in "The Tell-Tale Heart" resembles that produced in Poe's "The Colloquy of Monos and Una," published two years earlier. In Monos' account of dying and passing into eternity, he prefaces his final experience with a sensory acuteness similar to that experienced by the narrator in "The Tell-Tale Heart." "The senses were unusually active," Monos reports, "though eccentrically so— . . ." [IV, 206]. As the five senses fade in death, they are not utterly lost but merge into a sixth—of simple duration:

Motion in the animal frame had fully ceased. No muscle quivered; no nerve thrilled; no artery throbbed. But there seemed to have sprung up in the brain . . . a mental pendulous pulsation. . . . By its aid I measured the irregularities of the clock upon the mantel, and of the watches of the attendants. . . . And this—this keen, perfect, self-existing sentiment of *duration* . . . this sixth sense, upspringing from the ashes of the rest, was the first obvious and certain step of the intemporal soul upon the threshold of the temporal Eternity. [IV, 209–10]

Likewise the old man in "The Tell-Tale Heart" listens as though paralyzed, unable either to move or to hear anything that will dissolve his fears. This resembles Monos' sensory intensity and the cessation of "motion in the animal frame." Also subjective time is prolonged, becomes partially divorced from objective measurement, and dominates it. The most significant similarity comes in the conclusion of the experience. The old man does not know it but he is undergoing the same dissolution as Monos. He waits in vain for his fear to subside because actually it is "Death" whose shadow is approaching him, and "it was the mournful influence of that shadow that caused him to feel" his destroyer within the room. Like Monos, beyond his normal senses he has arrived at a "sixth sense," which is at first duration and then death.

But if the old man is nearing death so too must be the narrator, who has felt the same "mortal terror" in his own bosom. This similarity serves to unify the story. In Poe's tales, extreme sensitivity of the senses usually signalizes approaching death, as in the case of Monos and of Roderick Usher. This "over acuteness" in "The Tell-Tale Heart," however, pertains chiefly to the murderer, while death comes to the man with the "vulture eye." By making the narrator dramatize his feelings in the old man, Poe draws these two motifs together. We must remember, writes one commentator upon the story, "that the criminal sought his own death in that of his victim, and that he had in effect become the man who now lies dead." [2] Symbolically this is true. The resurgence of the beating heart shows that the horrors within himself, which the criminal attempted to identify with the old man and thus destroy, still live. In the death of the old man he sought to kill a part of himself, but his "demons" could not be exorcised through murder, for he himself is their destined victim.

From this point of view, the theme of "The Tell-Tale Heart" is self-destruction through extreme subjectivity marked paradoxically by both an excess of sensitivity and temporal solipsism. How seriously Poe could take this relativity of time and experience is evident in the poetic philosophy of his *Eureka* (1849). There time is extended almost infinitely into the life-cycle of the universe, but that cycle itself is only one heartbeat of God, who is the ultimate subjectivity. Romantically, indeed, Poe goes even further in the conclusion to *Eureka* and sees individual

---

[2] Patrick F. Quinn, *The French Face of Edgar Poe* (Carbondale, Illinois, 1957), p. 236. Quinn makes this identity the theme of the story, without describing the full sensory patterns upon which it is based.

man becoming God, enclosing reality within himself, and acting as his own creative agent. In this state, distinction between subjective and objective fades: "the sense of individual identity will be gradually merged in the general consciousness" [XVI, 314]. Destruction then becomes self-destruction, the madman and his victim being aspects of the same universal identity. Death not only is self-willed but takes on some of the sanctity of creative and hence destructive Deity. The heartbeat of the red slayer and the slain merge in Poe's metaphysical speculations as well as in the denouement of a horror story.

This extreme subjectivity, moreover, leaves the ethical problem of "The Tell-Tale Heart" unresolved. In the opening paragraph of the story is foreshadowed an issue of good and evil connected with the speaker's madness: "I heard all things in the heaven and in the earth. I heard many things in hell. How, then, am I mad?" [V, 88]. To be dramatically functional such an issue must be related to the murder. The only outward motivation for the murder is irritation at the "vulture eye." It is the evil of the eye, not the old man (whom he "loved"), that the murderer can no longer live with, and to make sure that it is destroyed he will not kill the man while he is sleeping. What the "Evil Eye" represents that it so arouses the madman we do not know, but since he sees himself in his companion the result is self-knowledge. Vision becomes insight, the "Evil Eye" an evil "I," and the murdered man a victim sacrificed to a self-constituted deity. In this story, we have undeveloped hints of the self-abhorrence uncovered in "William Wilson" and "The Imp of the Perverse."

Poe also has left unresolved the story's ultimate degree of subjectivity. No objective setting is provided; so completely subjective is the narration that few or no points of alignment with the external world remain. From internal evidence, we assume the speaker to be mad, but whether his words constitute a defense before some criminal tribunal or the complete fantasy of a madman there is no way of ascertaining.[3] The

---

[3] Despite lack of objective evidence, "The Tell-Tale Heart" bears much resemblance to a dream. The narrator acknowledges that the murdered man's shriek was such as occurs in dreams, and his memory of approaching the old man's bed upon eight successive midnights has the quality of a recurring nightmare. Poe frequently couples madness and dreaming, often with the variant "opium dreams," as in "Ligeia" and "The Fall of the House of Usher." "The Black Cat," a companion piece published the same year as "The Tell-Tale Heart" (1843), opens with an explicit denial of both madness and dreaming. The introductory paragraph of "Eleonora" (1842) runs the complete course of madness—dreams—death—good and evil: "Men have called me mad; but the question is not yet settled, whether madness is or is not the loftiest intelligence: whether much that is glorious, whether all that is profound, does not spring from disease of thought—from *moods* of mind exalted at the expense of the general intellect. They who dream by day are cognizant of many things which escape those who dream only by night. In their gray visions they obtain glimpses of

difference, however, is not material, for the subjective experience, however come by, *is* the story. Psychologically, the lengthening concentration upon internal states of being has divorced the murderer first from normal chronology and finally from relationship with the "actual" world. The result, in Beach's words, is "disintegration of the psychological complex." The victim images himself as another and recoils from the vision. Seeing and seen eye become identical and must be destroyed.

---

eternity, and thrill, in awaking, to find that they have been upon the verge of the great secret. In snatches, they learn something of the wisdom which is of good, and more of the mere knowledge which is of evil" (I, 96).

Poe's Detective God

by Robert Daniel

I

"Truth, Sir, is a cow which will yield such people no more milk, and so they are gone to milk the bull."

Samuel Johnson

The centenary of Poe's death in 1849 evoked new tributes to the keenness of his intelligence, in proof of which his detective stories were freely cited. Forty years earlier he had been called the inventor of the detective story, by no less an authority than Arthur Conan Doyle; but this claim has since been challenged. Dorothy L. Sayers' *Omnibus of Crime* begins with four "primitives," from pre-Christian times, though under "The Modern Detective Story" it includes none earlier than "The Mystery of Marie Rogêt." At any rate we may safely say that Poe invented the detective, so far as fiction is concerned, as well as his characteristic milieu. Much has been written about the influence of this character, C. Auguste Dupin, upon subsequent literary sleuths. Yet something can be added on Poe's creation of him, on the significance of his residing in Paris, and on the supernatural impressiveness of his exploits. If detectives work miracles, this fact will help to answer a question much debated lately: Why are detective stories popular?

One of Paul Elmer More's Shelburne Essays[1] contains a hint that may be applied to the analysis of Dupin. More discusses only such stories of Poe's as "The Fall of the House of Usher" which overtly employ supernatural events, as many of Hawthorne's do. He sees the origin of their supernaturalism in the Pre-Revolutionary imagination, which, largely Puritan, had been obsessed by phantasms of witches and

---

"Poe's Detective God" by Robert Daniel. From Furioso *VI (Summer, 1951), pp. 45–52. Copyright © 1951 by Reed Whittemore. Reprinted by permission of Reed Whittemore.*

[1] "The Origins of Hawthorne and Poe," *First Series* (New York: G. P. Putnam's Sons, 1907), pp. 51–70.

devils. After the relaxation of religious belief at the end of the eighteenth century, so More believed, these terrors persisted in stories of the weird. The popularity of Hawthorne and Poe thus stemmed from the substitution of fearsome symbols for Christian myths that were no longer literally believed.

But are not the Dupin stories also stories of the supernatural? In one important respect More's idea is incomplete: it finds no deities among the characters with which it deals, although religions center on gods, demi-gods, or super-men at least. If Dupin is rightly understood as a worker of miracles, the empty niche in More's pantheon will then be filled. Dupin is a sort of secular god; and Poe's Romanticism, which led him to exalt the gifted individual while discrediting the institutions of society in the persons of the police, produced the most enduring religious substitute in the imagination of what has been called A Century of Hero-Worship. The detective story, which has marched into our century almost unaltered in the deepest respects, probably arouses the same feelings now as one hundred years ago.

When the publication of "The Murders in the Rue Morgue" in *Graham's Magazine* for April, 1841, introduced the modern detective, Poe was well known for other kinds of writing. In imagining Dupin, he had only to combine three elements that he had already developed in his earlier work: his fancied genius for solving puzzles, the love of paradox that characterizes his reviewing, and the decadent aristocrat (the prototype being Roderick Usher) who dominates the tales of horror and terror. These three characters—Dupin, the Usher-hero, and Edgar A. Poe the Critic—are essentially the same personage.

The kinship of Dupin and Usher is easily seen, but it is not generally recognized how profoundly Poe's criticism relies on paradox, in the sense of statements contrary to received opinions. Poe's view of society as organized stupidity is reflected in the French sentence with which he opened his review of Longfellow's *Ballads and Tales,* and which appealed to him so strongly that he used it again in "The Purloined Letter." It may be loosely translated as, "Whatever the majority believes is probably nonsense" [XI, 64; VI, 28]. Guided by this maxim, he centered most of his reviews on ridicule of a popular idea. In 1845 he denies that the drama has declined. Elsewhere he denies that the imagination is creative, that there is a difference between theory and practice, and that a critic should ever praise a book [XV, 13n]. His review of Macaulay's *Essays* perfectly exemplifies the habit, which virtually became Poe's trademark as a critic: "Macaulay," it begins, "has obtained a reputation which, although deservedly great, is yet in a remarkable measure undeserved" [X, 156].

Poe's longer essays are equally dissident. "The Rationale of Verse" starts with an assault upon all who have presumed to speak on the

subject of prosody. In explaining how "a thousand profound scholars"
can have been wrong, Poe maintains among other things that they have
been misled by the simplicity of the subject [XIV, 209]—a paradox
which reappears in "The Murders in the Rue Morgue" and is of course
the foundation of "The Purloined Letter." ("Perhaps it is the very simplicity of the thing that puts you at fault," observes Dupin [VI, 29].)
Passing to Poe's description of how he wrote "The Raven," we find
him maintaining that the writing of a poem has "the precision and
rigid consequence of a mathematical problem" [XIV, 195]—which con-
tradicts not only the common notion but also the description of the
poetic mood in Poe's best-known essay, "The Poetic Principle." The
burden of the latter is the enforcement of two paradoxes: that long
poems do not exist, and that the object of poetry is not truth. The
public was expected to be startled by both these propositions, as is
plain from Poe's remark that "by being generally condemned as falsi-
ties they will not be essentially damaged as truths" [XIV, 268].

So it is seen that Poe's criticism reflects his sense of alienation from
society. For their lack of understanding he repaid his contemporaries
with scorn. It remains to show how this cast of his mind influenced his
later fiction. There are several ways in which the detective stories appear to be extensions of Poe's criticism. As a reviewer he is very much
the sleuth-hound; he ferrets out plagiarism, and hunts down writers
guilty of bad taste, confused thinking, or the murder of the language.
Contrariwise, the detective stories may be regarded as essays in criticism
—Dupin's adverse criticism of the bumbling policemen, whom he
treats much as Poe treated most of the authors whom he reviewed.
Above all, as the structure of "The Murders in the Rue Morgue"
shows, when Poe turned to the detective story he was mainly concerned to dramatize a superior character, the detective, much as he had
dramatized himself in his reviews. He would often try out particular
paradoxes there and then rework them round the figure of Dupin; but
the grand paradox is the transformation of a human character into a
god.

II

*"The mass of the people regard as profound only him who
suggests pungent contradictions of the general idea."*

                                                    C. Auguste Dupin

It required effrontery for Poe to have Dupin disparage contradictions
of what the majority believes. The quoted sentence gives the correct
account of Dupin's reputation for profundity, while at the same time

suggesting that he follows only such views as are commonly held to be true. Itself a paradox, it affords no contrast to the paradoxes and contradictions out of which the figure of Dupin is woven. When we analyze the Dupin stories in the light of this dictum, we are led to make three observations: first, Poe is concerned above all to project a remarkable character, his own alter ego; second, the character is remarkable largely because of his supernatural exploits, most of which are made credible by trickery; and third, his function in society is one that allowed Poe to dominate society imaginatively, when in fact society pretty much rejected him.

The characterization of Dupin in "The Murders in the Rue Morgue" depends upon contradiction from the start. Like Usher he is an invalid. Nobly born but with his energy destroyed by the shipwreck of his fortunes, he inhabits a "time-eaten and grotesque mansion" [IV, 151], ventures forth only at night, and passes his days in reading and dreaming. Yet though unable to cope with the ordinary exigencies of life, he solves crimes that have baffled the trained intelligence of the Paris police. His success seems intuitive, but really results from the methodical analysis of data. Poe has him refer to his peculiar faculty as that of "educated thought."

Poe's absorption in this character explains the odd form of the story, with its long opening essay which delays the plot. Poe is developing the character of "The Analyst," as he calls him; Dupin is the Analyst *par excellence*; the discovery that an orang-utan has committed the murders is but an illustration of his powers. The introductory section, which modern critics find intrusive and unaccountable, was in 1841 of paramount importance to the success of the idea that a debilitated amateur would triumph where the police had failed. At that time it was not known that the amateur can regularly beat the professional on his own ground.

The preliminary paradoxes, in other words, put the reader in a frame of mind where he will believe anything. He first encounters an extended and—it must be admitted—specious demonstration that checkers is a more profound game than chess; checkers more decidedly tasks "the higher powers of the reflective intellect." Whereas winning at chess is a mere matter of paying attention, games of checkers are won by "some strong exertion of the intellect," such as putting oneself in one's opponent's place. Before the reader can object that the successful chess-player must do the same, he is hurried into a discussion of the frivolity of chess as compared with whist. Here is found the slighting reference to common opinion: to remember the cards and follow the rules "are points commonly regarded as the sum total of good playing." But the Analyst, we are told, wins because of the inferences he can draw from the expressions and actions of the other players [IV, 146–49].

All is now in readiness for the introduction of Dupin. The first incident in the story shows his ability to read men's thoughts, as though they "wore windows in their bosoms": during a walk, the narrator is immersed in a reverie about an actor, and Dupin reads his mind. The narrator's comment on this feat deserves attention:

"Dupin," said I, gravely, "this is beyond my comprehension. I do not hesitate to say that I am amazed, and can scarcely credit my senses." [IV, 153]

Such language is the language appropriate to miracle and, in fact, a miracle has just been wrought. Outbursts of this kind are from now on to accompany the fictional detective's discoveries; they are one of the hardiest devices that Poe gave to the form. Dr. Watson is particularly prone to them. Dupin's feat scarcely goes beyond the possible— though some strain may be felt in the transitions from "stereotomy" to atomies to the theories of Epicurus; but what makes the incident miraculous is that it is supposed to be representative. That is, we are led to feel that Dupin can read thoughts whenever he chooses, not only when the reverie has been specially arranged for discovery, but always.

The same applies to Dupin's discovery that the women in the Rue Morgue were slain by an orang-utan. What outrages probability is not the process of his reasoning but the phenomena that he reasons about. The police arrest a bank clerk named Le Bon. An oddity of the witnesses' testimony, however, shows Dupin that the crimes have not been done by a human being: though all agree that one of the suspects spoke French, all differ on the language of the other. Conceivably, Paris being the cosmopolitan place that it is, a murderer's voice could be overheard by four foreigners in addition to a normal quota of Frenchmen. But is it likely that the "fiendish jabberings of the brute" would be mistaken for Russian by the Italian, for German by the Englishman, for English by the Spaniard, for French by the Hollander, for Spanish by one Frenchman, and for Italian by another? We might expect at least one witness to exclaim: "It sounded precisely like the fiendish jabberings of a brute!"

At all events the police arrest Le Bon and, as foils to the sagacity of Dupin, overlook several other improbable clues. The windows of the bedroom not only fasten by secret springs but also appear to be nailed down. Dupin, however, noticing that one of the nails is broken in two, readily opens the window by manipulating its spring. The window stood open when the murderer arrived, afforded him a means of escape, and locked by the spring after he had departed. Presumably it shut of its own accord, since an orang-utan would not have bothered.

Though first on the premises, the police also ignore the gold coins that are scattered about, a greasy ribbon from which Dupin deduces the murderer's companion to have been a Maltese sailor, and, most astonishing of all, a tuft of coarse hair clenched in the fingers of the murdered Mme. L'Espanaye. Even the narrator can see that it is not the hair of a human being.

From the detecting standpoint Dupin's fancy reasoning about the languages and the window-fastening is made supererogatory by his possession of the tuft of hair. These passages lead not to the identification of the murderer but to the establishment of Dupin's omniscience. And such was Poe's main design in writing the story.

A year and a half later, in a magazine called *The Ladies' Companion,* Poe brought out "The Mystery of Marie Rogêt." Labeled a sequel to the first Dupin story, it resembles it in many ways. The narrator, though too stupid to follow Dupin's deductions except at a distance, discusses coincidence with the same easy mastery of paradox that he showed in his observations on chess and whist. Dupin has progressed from Monsieur to Chevalier, an archaic title of nobility that sets him still farther apart from the mass of men. His supercilious indolence is more marked than ever, yet the police have by this time come to regard his ability as "little less than miraculous" [V, 3].

The important difference between the stories is that Marie Rogêt was a thin disguise for Mary Rogers, the name of a real girl whose body had been found floating in the Hudson River on 28 July 1841. Dupin's powers were now to be displayed in the solution of an actual crime, the clues to which had not been arranged by his creator.

Dupin's solution, which has been analyzed in an article by W. K. Wimsatt, Jr.,[2] proves to have been a triumph of error. Living in Philadelphia at the time, Poe worked from newspaper accounts of the affair. His solution hinted at the guilt of the girl's lover (another sailor!). Though the case has never been cleared of mystery, the evidence of Poe's blunder is his revision of the story, which appeared in *Tales by Edgar A. Poe* in 1845. By then Poe had moved to New York and had probably heard discussions of the case that made him change his mind. Wimsatt's comparison of the two versions shows that the reasoning which had first brought the lover under suspicion, leads in the second edition to the conclusion that Mary died accidentally, as the result of an abortion.

One other story completes the saga of Dupin. In "The Purloined Letter" (1845) he is as supercilious as ever: "The Parisian police," he

---

[2] "Poe and the Beautiful Cigar Girl," *American Literature* XX (1948), pp. 305–12.

allows, "are exceedingly able in their way" [VI, 39].[3] Though most
people suppose that the way to hide a document is to conceal it, Dupin
shows that it is better to leave it in plain sight. The paradox of The
Obvious Hiding-Place is hedged about by demonstrations that mathe-
maticians cannot reason and that in climbing it is easier to get up
than to come down. Dupin finds the letter by identifying himself with
the intellect of the purloiner, and his feat is again accompanied by the
language of miracle. At his success, the narrator tells us,

> I was astounded. The Prefect appeared absolutely thunder-stricken. For
> some minutes he remained speechless and motionless, looking incredu-
> lously at my friend with open mouth, and eyes that seemed starting from
> their sockets . . . [VI, 39].

Besides these likenesses, "The Purloined Letter" presents Dupin in a
new relation. It is suggested towards the end of the story that he is a
savior and, doubtless, had Poe continued his saga, this strain would
have been developed. Only a hint of it actually occurs, but from this
hint much may be concluded about Poe's attitude towards his detective,
and hence towards himself. When Dupin retrieves the letter, he dares
not do so openly, for, as he explains, the Minister's desperate character
placed him in grave danger. "Had I made the wild attempt you suggest,
I might never have left the Ministerial presence alive. The good people
of Paris might have heard of me no more" [VI, 51]. Dupin is both far
withdrawn from humanity and at its service. His talents expose him to
the risk of being sacrificed for the welfare of the herd, whom he patron-
izes.

Since Poe wrote no more stories about Dupin, the development of
the detective as sacrificial victim was left to Conan Doyle. It will be
noted that Sherlock Holmes, whose "people" are the citizens of London, inherited from Dupin the milieu of the great metropolis. Does
this likeness not serve to introduce one further paradox, of which Poe
could not have been entirely aware? The city is the typical setting for
realistic novels; and no fact about the detective story is odder than its
emergence at a time when the public was demanding realism above all
other qualities in its fiction. Though the trappings of the detective
story—its dialogue and descriptions, its obsession with fingerprints
and microscopes—are realistic to the point of literalness, in the characteristic example of the form two fantastic elements stand out against

[3] The police get hard usage in the Dupin stories. They fail to find the purloined
letter because of the minuteness of their search; they scrutinize every chair-rung, etc.
Yet they are the same who could not find the hidden nail and other inconspicuous
clues in "The Murders in the Rue Morgue." Poe has it both ways.

their commonplace surroundings: the bizarre nature of the crime, and the intuitive solution by an amateur. In reality, as the newspapers daily attest, most murders are committed by such humdrum means as stabbing or gunshot, and all but an isolated few of the solutions are effected by the methodical methods of the professional police. A solution by an amateur is rarer than an eclipse of the sun.

Chronology of Important Dates

	Poe	Historical and Cultural Events
1809	Born.	James Madison becomes fourth President. Darwin, Tennyson, and Lincoln born. Irving's *Knickerbocker's History* published.
1812	Enters household of John Allan.	America at war with England. Napoleon retreats from Moscow.
1815	Family in London for five years.	Battle of Waterloo. *North American Review* established.
1827	Leaves University of Virginia, publishes *Tamerlane and Other Poems*.	Niepce secures first camera image. Cooper's *The Prairie* published.
1830	Dismissed from West Point.	Joseph Smith organizes Mormon Church. Audubon's *Birds of America* and Lyell's *Principles of Geology* published.
1833	Wins contest with "MS Found in a Bottle."	British Factory Act passed. Carlyle's *Sartor Resartus* published.
1835– 1837	Edits *Southern Literary Messenger*.	Samuel Colt invents revolver. Victoria ascends the throne. Martin Van Buren becomes eighth President. Emerson's *Nature,* Dickens' *Oliver Twist,* and Hawthorne's *Twice-Told Tales* published. Mark Twain, Bret Harte, and William Dean Howells born.
1840	Publishes *Tales of the Grotesque and Arabesque.*	Harrison and Tyler elected. Victoria marries Albert. Brook Farm and *The Dial* established.

1845	Publishes *The Raven and Other Poems;* joins *Broadway Journal.*	Texas annexed. James K. Polk becomes eleventh President. Thoreau goes to Walden. Repeal of British Corn Laws.
1847	Death of Virginia Poe; beginning of decline.	America at war with Mexico. Brontë sisters publish *Wuthering Heights* and *Jane Eyre.* Longfellow's *Evangeline* and Melville's *Omoo* published.
1848	Publishes *Eureka.*	Mill's *Principles of Political Economy* and Marx and Engel's *Communist Manifesto* published. Franklin finds Northwest Passage. Gold discovered in California.
1849	Dies.	Zachary Taylor becomes twelfth President. Ruskin's *Seven Lamps of Architecture* and Thoreau's *A Week on the Concord and Merrimack Rivers* published. Sarah Orne Jewett born.

Notes on the Editor and Contributors

WILLIAM L. HOWARTH is Assistant Professor of English at Princeton University. He has published an essay on Stephen Crane, edited *A Thoreau Gazetteer* (1970), and compiled a forthcoming catalogue of Thoreau's manuscripts.

ROBERT DANIEL is Professor of English at Kenyon College, Gambier, Ohio. He served as Fulbright Professor at the University of Athens in 1954–55, and he has edited three widely-used college texts: *Theme and Form* (1956, rev. 1962), *The Written Word* (1960), and *A Contemporary Rhetoric* (1967).

JAMES W. GARGANO is Professor of English at Washington and Jefferson College, Washington, Pa. A Fulbright lecturer at Caen in 1964–65, he has written several essays on the fiction of Hawthorne, James, and Poe.

JOSEPH M. GARRISON, JR. is Associate Professor of English at Mary Baldwin College, Staunton, Va. His published work in American literature ranges from John Burroughs to the poetry of Edward Taylor.

CLARK GRIFFITH is Professor of English at the University of Iowa. Author of *The Long Shadow: Emily Dickinson's Tragic Poetry* (1964), and of essays on Whitman, Frost, and Wallace Stevens, he was Visiting Professor at the American University of Cairo in 1966–67.

JOHN S. HILL is Professor of English at Illinois State University. He has written articles on various American authors, including Poe, Mark Twain, and Thomas Wolfe.

JOHN LAUBER is Associate Professor of English at the University of Alberta. Author of *Sir Walter Scott* (1967), he has also published essays on Hawthorne, American innocence, and the poetry of Lord Byron.

HARRY LEVIN is Irving Babbitt Professor of Comparative Literature at Harvard University. Besides *The Power of Blackness: Hawthorne, Poe, Melville* (1958), he has written books on Joyce, Stendahl, Balzac, Marlowe, and Shakespeare. His most recent publications are *Why Literary Criticism Is Not an Exact Science* (1968) and *The Myth of the Golden Age in the Renaissance* (1969).

TERENCE MARTIN is Professor of English at Indiana University. His writings include *The Instructed Vision* (1961), *Nathaniel Hawthorne* (1965), and essays on Irving and James. In 1959–60 he was Visiting Professor of American Literature at Dijon.

STEPHEN L. MOONEY is Professor of English at the University of Tennessee at Martin. Founder and editor of the *Tennessee Poetry Journal*, he is the author of *Shakespeare's Father and Other Poems* (1949), *News from the South* (1966), and *The Grave of the Dwarf* (1968).

CHARLES O'DONNELL is Associate Professor of English at the University of Michigan. He has written essays on Cooper and Hawthorne, and since 1966 he has served as a professional adviser to the Educational Testing Service.

E. ARTHUR ROBINSON is Professor of English at the University of Rhode Island. His published work includes studies of Meredith, Hawthorne, Poe, and Thoreau.

DONALD BARLOW STAUFFER is Associate Professor of English at the State University of New York at Albany. Author of several articles on Poe's prose style, he has contributed to the annual *International Bibliography* of the Modern Language Association since 1965.

I. M. WALKER is Lecturer in American Literature at Manchester University, Manchester, England. He has published various essays on nineteenth-century authors; recently he completed a forthcoming book on Mark Twain. He has also served as Visiting Professor at the University of Missouri.

WILLIAM CARLOS WILLIAMS (1883–1963), a leading figure in twentieth-century American literature, published numerous volumes of poetry, fiction, drama, and critical prose. For half a century he also practiced pediatric medicine in Rutherford, New Jersey, his lifelong home.

YVOR WINTERS was Albert Guerard Professor of English at Stanford University at the time of his death in 1968. He wrote several volumes of poetry, a biography of E. A. Robinson (1946), and a series of important critical works: *Primitivism and Decadence* (1937), *Maule's Curse* (1938), *The Anatomy of Nonsense* (1943); collected as *In Defense of Reason* (1947).

Selected Bibliography

Collections

Carlson, Eric W., ed. *The Recognition of Edgar Allan Poe* (Ann Arbor: University of Michigan Press, 1966). An extensive selection of criticism, 1829–1965.

Regan, Robert, ed. *Poe: A Collection of Critical Essays* (Englewood Cliffs, N.J.: Prentice-Hall, Inc., 1967). Important general essays; several articles on specific tales.

Woodson, Thomas, ed. *Twentieth-Century Interpretations of The Fall of the House of Usher* (Englewood Cliffs, N.J.: Prentice-Hall, Inc., 1969). Differing views of one tale.

Essays

Baym, Nina, "The Function of Poe's Pictorialism," *South Atlantic Quarterly* LXV (1966), 46–54. Patterns in fictional setting and description; their relation to Poe's ideas on imagination.

Blair, Walter, "Poe's Conception of Incident and Tone in the Tale," *Modern Philology* XLI (1944), 228–40. Analysis of fictional "theory," with extended application to "The Masque of the Red Death."

Dedmond, Francis B., " 'The Cask of Amontillado' and the War of the Literati," *Modern Language Quarterly* XV (1954), 137–46. How the tale's historical context affects its meaning.

Hirsch, David H., "The Pit and the Apocalypse," *Sewanee Review* LXXVI (1968), 632–52. Poe's style permits "The Pit and the Pendulum" to transcend its conventions of Gothic horror.

Hassel, J. Woodrow, Jr., "The Problem of Realism in 'The Gold Bug'," *American Literature* XXV (1953), 179–92. The philosophical implications of Legrand's puzzle-solving.

Moldenhauer, Joseph J., "Murder as a Fine Art: Connections Between Poe's Aesthetics, Psychology, and Moral Vision," *PMLA* LXXXIII (1968), 284–97. Poe's characters—artists, murderers, detectives—seek the common goal of Unity.

Vanderbilt, Kermit, "Art and Nature in 'The Masque of the Red Death'," *Nineteenth-Century Fiction* XXII (1968), 379–89. Interprets the tale in the light of Poe's emerging ideas, ca. 1842.

TWENTIETH CENTURY
INTERPRETATIONS

MAYNARD MACK, *Series Editor*
Yale University

NOW AVAILABLE
Collections of Critical Essays
ON

ADVENTURES OF HUCKLEBERRY FINN
ALL FOR LOVE
THE AMBASSADORS
ARROWSMITH
AS YOU LIKE IT
BLEAK HOUSE
THE BOOK OF JOB
BOSWELL'S LIFE OF JOHNSON
THE CASTLE
CORIOLANUS
DOCTOR FAUSTUS
DON JUAN
DUBLINERS
THE DUCHESS OF MALFI
ENDGAME
EURIPIDES' ALCESTIS
THE FALL OF THE HOUSE OF USHER
A FAREWELL TO ARMS
THE FROGS
GRAY'S ELEGY
THE GREAT GATSBY
GULLIVER'S TRAVELS
HAMLET
HARD TIMES
HENRY IV, PART ONE
HENRY IV, PART TWO
HENRY V
THE ICEMAN COMETH
INVISIBLE MAN
JULIUS CAESAR
KEATS'S ODES
LIGHT IN AUGUST

(continued on next page)

Lord Jim
Major Barbara
Measure for Measure
The Merchant of Venice
Moll Flanders
Molloy, Malone Dies, The Unnamable
Much Ado about Nothing
The Nigger of the "Narcissus"
Oedipus Rex
The Old Man and the Sea
Pamela
A Passage to India
The Playboy of the Western World
Poe's Tales
The Portrait of a Lady
A Portrait of the Artist as a Young Man
The Praise of Folly
Pride and Prejudice
The Rainbow
The Rape of the Lock
The Rime of the Ancient Mariner
Robinson Crusoe
Romeo and Juliet
Samson Agonistes
The Scarlet Letter
Sir Gawain and the Green Knight
Songs of Innocence and of Experience
Sons and Lovers
The Sound and the Fury
The Tempest
Tess of the D'Urbervilles
Tom Jones
To the Lighthouse
Twelfth Night
The Turn of the Screw and Other Tales
Utopia
Vanity Fair
Walden
The Waste Land
Women in Love
Wuthering Heights